DAN TOOMBS
THE CURRY GUY
CHICKEN

DAN TOOMBS

THE CURRY GUY
CHICKEN

**Deliciously Spiced Recipes from
South and Southeast Asia**

Photography by Kris Kirkham

quadrille

CONTENTS

Preface   6
Let's Get Started   8

Starters and Snacks   10
Korean Fried Chicken
    Kimbap   13
Da Lat Chicken Pizza   15
Chicken Majestic   16
Dragon Chicken   18
Punjabi Chicken Samosas   21
Chicken Samosa Cups   22
Pandan Chicken   24
Baked Tandoori
    Chicken Wings   26

Karahi Cooking   28
About the Karahi Recipes   30
Chicken Karahi with
    Chillies and Garlic   33
Butter Chicken Karahi   35
White Chicken Karahi
(Korma)   36
Chicken Keema Karahi   38
Chicken Jalfrezi Karahi   41
Chicken Bhuna Karahi   43
Chicken Chole Karahi   44
Chicken Saag Karahi   47
    Black Pepper
Chicken Karahi   48
Chicken Namkeen Karahi   51

Chicken Curries, Stews and Sauce-based Dishes   52
Jeera (Cumin)
Chicken Curry   55
Ayam Rica Rica   57
Soto Ayam   58
Chicken Pallipalayam   60
South Indian Chicken
    Drumstick Curry   63
Bangalore Green Chilli
    Chicken Curry   65
Chicken Shahi Korma   66
White Chicken Shahi
    Kofta Korma   68
Chicken Changezi   71
Kari Ayam Jawa   73
Korean Spicy Ramen   74
Szechuan Chicken   76
Goan-Style Chicken
    Vindaloo   79
Punjabi Ginger
    Chicken Curry   81
Vietnamese Whole
    Boiled Chicken   82
Chicken Rogan Josh
    (Chicken Roghani)   84
Korean Chicken Stew   87
Sri Lankan Chicken Curry   89
General Tso's Chicken   91
Thai Chicken Biryani   92
Chicken Haleem   94
Chicken Rendang   97

Frying and Stir-fries   98

Chicken Chapli Kebabs   100
Crispy Indonesian
  Fried Chicken   102
Chicken Jali Kebabs   105
Korean Miso Chicken   106
Kolkata Chicken Chaap   108
Chicken Shami Kebabs   111

Wraps and Sandwiches   112

Bánh Mì   115
Tandoori Chicken Burger   117
Chicken Shami Bun Kebabs   118
Chicken Frankie   121
Keema Pav   122

Barbecue   124

Setting Up Your Barbecue   126
Chicken Bulgogi   128
Grilled Butter Chicken   130
Indonesian Chicken Sate   133
Kagzhi Kebabs   135
Malai Chicken Seekh Kebabs   136
Gilafi Chicken Seekh Kebabs   138
Honey Roast
  Tandoori Chicken   141
Vietnamese-Style
  Rotisserie Chicken   143
Chicken Yakitori   145
Indonesian Grilled Chicken   146
Chicken Lilit   148

Basics, Accompaniments and Sides   150

Indian Hotel (Restaurant)
  Batch Gravies   152
Tomato and Onion Gravy   154
Makhani Gravy   155
Hariyali (Green) Gravy   156
White Gravy   158
Onion Gravy   159
Chicken Stock   160
Garam Masala   161
Garlic and Ginger
  (and Chilli) Paste   161
Chicken Floss   162
Nu'ó'c Châ'm   163
Thai Cucumber Salad   163
Steamed White
  Basmati Rice   164
Instant Parathas   164
Naans   165
Rumali Rotis   166
Indonesian Rice Cakes   167
All-Purpose Tandoori
  Marinade   168
Mint Raita   168
Punjabi Tomato Chutney   169
Green Chilli and
  Coriander Chutney   169

Suppliers   170
Index   171
Acknowledgements   175

PREFACE

The fact that you are reading this right now means you probably love deliciously spiced chicken as much as I do. If that's the case, then this book is for you! I had a lot of fun researching and developing these chicken recipes, from steaming and simmering, to grilling and frying the popular bird. You will find a good selection of chicken recipes from around the Indian subcontinent and Southeast Asia that are quite easy to prepare and taste incredible. There are also a few fusion chicken recipes that I simply had to include.

While pork and beef tend to be off the menu in many countries for religious reasons, chicken is popular the world over. Although I do hope to write further books focusing on different meats, chicken simply seemed to be the best place to start. Chicken can be cooked in so many mouthwatering ways as it is neutral in flavour and mixes well with the complementary ingredients that are cooked with it. You are going to find some delicious examples, from crispy fried to stir-fried, and steamed and grilled and roasted…

Of course, loving a good curry as I do, you'll find plenty of those in the following pages, but I have also delved into many more chicken preparations. Some of my test cooks didn't make it past our dinner table as I only wanted to feature the best! These recipes have all been tried and tested, some many times in my own home kitchen, and they are the recipes that got the best feedback from my family and friends, as well as the readers of my blog.

If you have one or more of my other cookbooks, you might wonder what could possibly be on offer in this book that I haven't already covered. No need to worry there, as I didn't want to just give you popular chicken recipes that were already featured in my previous books! There are so many recipes and cooking styles that just

didn't fit the spec of the earlier books, so you're going to have a lot of new recipes and flavours to try. What's more, I think you might like this selection of chicken recipes just as much, if not better than those I have already put out there!

In addition to the many recipes from around Southeast Asia that I knew needed to be in this book, I decided to put a special emphasis on two areas. The first is traditional karahi cooking. I am often asked through comments on my blog and on social media for proper karahi curry recipes like you find at so many good restaurants, and you're going to get them here! Some of these curries are quite oil heavy, just like they are in India and Pakistan, but they are worth the calories. If cooking with a lot of oil doesn't appeal to you, no worries. I have given advice on pages 30–1 on how to amend the recipes for your own taste preference and diet.

Another subject I have wanted to cover for a while is Indian hotel (restaurant) style gravies. You'll find these in the Basic, Accompaniments and Sides section at the end of the book because you won't actually be needing them to cook any of the curries. You will learn how to make and use them though, and they might just take your curries to the next level!

These batch-cooked gravies are just like those used at the best Indian hotel restaurants and they will cut your cooking time down substantially with so many curries, not just those featured in this book.

I hope you enjoy cooking and trying this new collection of chicken recipes as much as we enjoyed finding and devouring them. If you have any questions about any of the recipes, please get in touch. I manage all of my own social media accounts, so if you ask a question, it will be me who answers. I'm @TheCurryGuy on X, Facebook, TikTok and Instagram and would love to hear from you.

LET'S GET STARTED

To help you find the recipes you want to try, I have labelled them with these badges.

Gluten-free: So many of the following recipes are traditionally made gluten-free. Some aren't, however, so I have clearly marked those that are with this badge. If you are on a gluten-free diet, then you probably already know to look for hidden gluten in common ingredients such as fish sauce and oyster sauce. This badge will help you find the recipes that are gluten-free or can easily be made so by using gluten-free options.

Quick: Look for this badge if you want to whip up a meal in minutes with little fuss.

Fermenting, marinating and soaking: Just follow the preparation instructions and let nature take its course. I have included this badge so that you know a little forward preparation will benefit the flavour of the dish.

Low and slow: Some recipes require a long cooking time. They are still easy though. Just let them simmer or roast, put your feet up and enjoy the meal when it's ready. Some of these might be best left for the weekend.

BBQ: There are many delicious recipes in the barbecue section of this book (pages 124–149) but there are also other recipes that will benefit from or are simply better cooked over fire. If you see this icon, you might want to consider doing just that.

Oil heavy: I wanted to stick to the traditional ways many Indian curries are made and that often means with a lot of oil, ghee or another fat. When you see this badge, you'll know you're getting the real deal but recipes are guides and not carved in stone. Feel free to use less oil if you like. The end results may not look or taste the same but will still be good. Often you might need to add a little stock or water if you want more gravy when reducing the amount of oil.

HOW TO USE THESE RECIPES

No recipe is set in stone! Recipes are guides or suggestions for how to best create a dish you know well or want to try to cook. So please feel free to use all of the following recipes as guides to your perfect dish.

The word 'your' is important because it's you who has to eat what you make. I have developed these recipes the way I like them but everyone has their own taste preferences and dietary requirements. If you make the recipes as written, you will get them as I learned to make them and enjoyed consuming them. There is absolutely no reason why you should stick exactly to the recipe though.

If you feel a recipe calls for too much or not enough chilli powder, for example, that's in your hands. Adjust the amounts of each of the ingredients called for in the recipes to your own taste and you will be much happier with the finished dish.

AN IMPORTANT NOTE ABOUT OIL AND GHEE

One of the questions I get asked most is: How do you make curries that have a shiny gleam to them like you find in so many restaurants? I'm afraid the answer to that one is oil, ghee and sometimes lard. Lots of it! In many of the traditional Indian recipes that follow, there is a heavy use of oil and ghee and, if you follow the recipe, you will get that characteristic glistening shine to the finished dish. I wanted to give you these recipes just as they're made in the Indian subcontinent but…

You don't have to use that much oil and/or ghee. Repeat: don't use that much fat if you want to eat lighter! The recipes will still work. In my book *The Curry Guy Light*, I showed that you can fry so many things without any oil at all, without much, if any, loss of flavour. This is not that book. In the following pages, you will find recipes that are heavy in oil, ghee and other fats, just like they are served at Indian street-food stalls and restaurants. For authenticity, make them as written or reduce the amount of fat used to your preference. You can cook a recipe that calls for 125ml (½ cup) of oil with as little as 1 tablespoon of oil. You might need to add some water or stock and the recipe will not look or taste the same but it will still be good.

Just like the Italians enjoy dipping their bread in olive oil, I can assure you there are few things better than dipping a naan or chapatti into the seasoned oil in these dishes. Admittedly, the olive oil used in the Med is a much healthier oil but these South

and Southeast Asian dishes were being served long before healthy diets.

One last thing… Some of the recipes call for coconut oil and mustard oil, which many people do not want to consume, again for health reasons. These oils add to the flavour and also give recipes a more traditional taste, but feel free to use a healthier oil if you prefer. That said, olive oil has a low smoke point and burns easily. It is bad for you and tastes bitter if heated over a high heat, so stay away from that.

HOW TO SERVE A DISH THAT'S OIL HEAVY

I think I should emphasize again here, right up front, that the majority of the recipes in this book are not substantially heavy in oil. However, the curries that are oilier than you might be used to are that way for a reason, as the hot oil helps break down the ingredients in the sauce in a way that just isn't possible with water, coconut milk or stock. You will notice if you make these oil-heavy curries as written that the oil separates from the sauce and floats to the top, adding amazing colour and gleam. When serving, dip your ladle or serving spoon deep into the sauce and bring it out. You will have a good ladleful of curry and a lot of the oil will ooze off back into the pan.

At street-food stalls and restaurants, the chefs often go back and skim off some of the shiny oil and drizzle it over the top of the plated curry for better presentation. Not convinced? You can always skim the majority of the oil off the top and discard it, but I hope you do find a good day when you want to spoil yourself and go for the real thing! Such curries are very rich in flavour and you only need a little with a naan, chapatti or rice to feel satisfied.

STARTERS AND SNACKS

Here are some outstanding starters and snacks that offer
the perfect way to start a meal. Some can also be served as
a lighter meal in their own right.

KOREAN FRIED CHICKEN KIMBAP
SERVES 4–6

Kimbaps are Korean-style sushi. I have listed a couple of popular veggie fillings to go with the fried chicken but use what you like. Things like sliced omelette and Korean pickled vegetables come to mind. Getting these kimbaps to look like they would in a restaurant takes practice, but even if yours end up a total mess, they will still taste great, so do make these! I promise, you'll love them. You could just dip them in soy sauce but I have given an optional Korean-style dip for you to try, too.

PREP TIME: 15 MINS, PLUS TIME TO COOK AND COOL THE RICE
COOKING TIME: 10 MINS

4 sheets of seaweed
1 tbsp sesame oil, plus extra for slicing
½ tsp salt
130g (1 cup) sushi rice, cooked as packet instructions, warm but not steaming hot
½ cucumber, peeled, seeded and thinly sliced lengthwise
1 medium carrot, peeled and julienned
1 tbsp sesame seeds

FOR THE CHICKEN

500g (1lb 2oz) chicken breasts or thighs, cut into long 1.25cm (½in) thick strips
250ml (1 cup) milk or buttermilk
3 garlic cloves, very finely chopped (minced)
1 tbsp light soy sauce or tamari
1 tbsp gochujang (Korean hot pepper paste)
30g (¼ cup) plain (all-purpose) flour
60g (1½ cups) panko breadcrumbs
Rapeseed (canola) oil, for frying

FOR THE DIPPING SAUCE (OPTIONAL)

70ml (¼ cup) light soy sauce or tamari
1 tbsp sesame oil
2 red finger chillies, finely chopped
1 tsp gochugaru (Korean hot pepper flakes, more or less to taste)
2 spring onions (scallions), thinly sliced into rings

In a mixing bowl, cover the chicken with the milk or buttermilk and let it soak while you prepare the other ingredients. After 20 minutes, pour out the milk, leaving the chicken damp. Add the chopped garlic, soy sauce and gochujang to the chicken and stir well to coat.

Now add the flour to the bowl and mix it right in with your hands to coat the chicken. It should look quite soupy. Pour the breadcrumbs onto a plate and roll the chicken in them to coat.

Heat about 10cm (4in) rapeseed (canola) oil in a frying pan (skillet) over a medium–high heat. Your oil is ready for frying when you stick a wooden chopstick or spatula in and thousands of little bubbles form around it on contact. Fry the chicken for 5–10 minutes, turning from time to time until crispy and golden brown. Be sure the chicken is cooked through and transfer the chicken with a slotted spatula to a wire rack to drip any excess oil. The internal temperature of cooked chicken is 74°C (165°F).

To make the kimbaps, place one of the seaweed sheets on a clean surface, shiny side down. Pour 2 teaspoons of the sesame oil and the salt over the rice and mix it in gently with your hands. Divide the cooked rice into four equal portions and place one of the portions on the seaweed sheet.

Looking at the sheet in front of you, you want to spread the rice thinly so that it goes right out to the sides of the sheet but leave about 2.5cm (1in) at the top (the bit furthest from you) without any rice. About 2.5cm (1in) from the bottom, place a row of the thinly sliced cucumber. Next to that, place a row of the julienned carrot. Next to the carrot, make a row of the fried chicken. From the bottom of the sheet, roll it over all the filling into a cylinder shape and squeeze it firmly. Then continue rolling until it's all rolled up. Repeat with the remaining ingredients.

Once all your kimbaps are prepared, rub them all over with the remaining sesame oil and sprinkle with the sesame seeds. Rub some sesame oil on the blade of a sharp knife. Then slowly and carefully slice the kimbaps into 1.25cm (½in) slices. You might need to oil your blade a few times to ease slicing.

To make the optional dipping sauce, simply whisk all the ingredients together and serve with your rolled kimbaps.

DA LAT CHICKEN PIZZA
SERVES 4–6

You are only limited by your own imagination with this hugely popular Vietnamese snack from the beautiful city of Da Lat. You can put whatever you like on the pizzas but this chicken version is a good start. This is pizza made with rice paper, which is normally cooked on a barbecue grate over hot coals. The pizzas are fun to make for all. Older kids love getting in there and cooking them. If you want to stay with a Vietnamese theme, you might like to cook the Vietnamese-style rotisserie chicken on page 143 and use some of that for this recipe, but any cooked chicken will do. Just don't add much liquid sauce before cooking as the rice paper will not get crispy.

PREP TIME: 5 MINS
COOKING TIME: 5 MINS

Oil, for brushing
12 rice paper rounds
700g (1lb 9oz) any cooked
    chicken, shredded

OPTIONAL GARNISHES
Mozzarella, grated
Mayonnaise
Sriracha sauce
Spring onions (scallions),
    finely chopped

To make the pizzas, scatter the coals for direct heat cooking (see page 127). Lightly spray or brush the grill with a little oil and place some rice paper rounds on it. Top with the shredded chicken and a little mozzarella if you like. Be sure to rotate the rice paper as it cooks so that it doesn't stick to the grill and try not to let the rice paper brown too much on the bottom.

Move it to a cooler part of the grill, if needed. You only want to make the rice paper crispy. The pizza is ready when the rice paper is crisp and the cheese, if using, has melted. Each pizza should only take a couple of minutes to prepare.

If you like, use squirty bottles to garnish the pizzas with some mayonnaise and sriracha, which are the traditional toppings. Serve right off the cooking grate when the cheese is melted and the meat heated through, garnished with the spring onions (scallions).

NOTE
You can also cook these pizzas in a lightly greased pan or non-stick pan over a medium–high heat on the stove.

CHICKEN MAJESTIC
SERVES 4

Chicken majestic is a popular chicken starter from southern India. It is similar to Chicken 65 but the chicken is cut into long strips rather than bite-sized tikka and is usually not coloured with red food colouring. There is also a little yoghurt added to the sauce to thicken it. It's known for its unique combination of spicy, tangy and slightly sweet flavours. While its exact origin is not clear, Chicken majestic is often associated with the city of Hyderabad. If you liked the Chicken 65 recipe in my previous books, you are going to love this too.

PREP TIME: 15 MINS
COOKING TIME: 15 MINS

600g (1lb 5oz) chicken breasts,
    sliced into long strips against
    the grain
125ml (½ cup) rapeseed
    (canola) oil

FOR THE MARINADE
3 tbsp buttermilk (optional)
½ tsp ground turmeric
1 tbsp garlic and ginger paste
1 level tsp salt
1 level tsp freshly ground
    black pepper
1 egg
2 tbsp rapeseed (canola) oil
40g (¼ cup) cornflour
    (cornstarch)

FOR THE CURRY
½ tsp cumin seeds
½ tsp fennel seeds
15 fresh or frozen curry leaves
½ red onion, very finely
    chopped
½ tsp ground turmeric
2–3 tsp Kashmiri chilli powder
    (or to taste)
2 tbsp garlic and ginger paste
3 green bird's eye chillies,
    finely chopped
3 spring onions (scallions),
    cut into 2.5cm (1in) pieces
70ml (¼ cup) natural yoghurt
1–2 tbsp light soy sauce
    or tamari
3 tbsp coriander (cilantro),
    finely chopped
Juice of 1 lime

Whisk the marinade ingredients together in a bowl until creamy and smooth. Add the chicken strips and allow to marinate for at least 30 minutes or overnight. The longer, the better.

When ready to cook, heat the oil in a large frying pan (skillet) or wok over a medium–high heat. Your oil is ready for cooking when you stick a wooden chopstick or spatula in and thousands of little bubbles form around it. Stir in the chicken and fry for about 6 minutes or until cooked through. As you are shallow-frying, it is important to stir regularly so that the chicken doesn't scorch in places. You want the chicken to be crispy, with a light golden exterior. Transfer the cooked chicken to a plate using a slotted spoon and set aside.

To make the curry, you need 2 tablespoons of clean oil. If you added the marinated chicken before the oil was hot enough, it might have a lot of excess flour floating in it. So either discard all but 2 tablespoons of the oil or discard it all if dirty, wipe your pan clean and start again.

Over a medium–high heat, stir in the cumin and fennel seeds and temper them in the oil for about 30 seconds. Then stir in the curry leaves and fry for a further 30 seconds. Add the chopped onion and fry to soften for a couple of minutes before stirring in the turmeric, chilli powder and garlic and ginger paste. Give this all a good stir and add the chopped chillies and spring onions (scallions). Add the yoghurt, soy sauce or tamari and then swirl it all into a thick and smooth sauce.

Add the fried chicken to this sauce and continue stirring until it is coated with the sauce. Add the chopped coriander (cilantro), squeeze in the lime juice and serve hot.

DRAGON CHICKEN
SERVES 4

There's no doubt about it, Indo-Chinese food is popular all over India and Dragon chicken is a firm favourite. This can be made in less than 30 minutes and is the perfect starter for any Indian or Chinese meal. Other vegetables can also be added, such as baby sweetcorn, sliced red onion or cherry tomatoes, but the recipe I have for you here is how it is most often served.

PREP TIME: 15 MINS
COOKING TIME: 15 MINS

FOR THE DRAGON CHICKEN

450g (1lb) chicken breasts, skinned and sliced into long strips against the grain
Rapeseed (canola) oil, for frying
12 cashews
4 garlic cloves, finely chopped
2.5cm (1in) piece of ginger, finely chopped
3 spring onions (scallions), finely chopped
1 tbsp dried chilli flakes (more or less to taste)
1 red (bell) pepper or the equivalent of red, green and yellow (bell) peppers, seeded and thinly sliced
2 tbsp light soy sauce or tamari
70ml (¼ cup) ketchup
1 tsp honey
70ml (¼ cup) chicken stock or water
1 tbsp Chinese or Thai chilli sauce or any chilli sauce you like
Salt and pepper, to taste
2 tbsp toasted sesame seeds, to serve

FOR THE MARINADE

1 egg
1 tbsp soy sauce or tamari
2 tbsp Chinese rice wine or dry sherry
1 tsp freshly ground black pepper
1 tsp salt
2 tbsp garlic and ginger paste
3 tbsp cornflour (cornstarch)

Whisk all the marinade ingredients in a mixing bowl until smooth with no lumps. Add the chicken strips and mix them into the marinade until completely coated. Allow to marinate for 30 minutes–2 hours or just carry on with the recipe. The longer marination time will add to the flavour.

When ready to cook, heat about 7.5cm (3in) of rapeseed (canola) oil in a large wok or frying pan (skillet) over a medium–high heat. The oil is ready for frying when thousands of little bubbles form around a wooden spatula or chopstick on contact with the oil. Carefully add the chicken strips to the oil and fry for a few minutes or until golden brown. Transfer to a plate and set aside. Discard all but about 3 tablespoons of the oil or filter it through a cloth to use for other frying.

Heat the remaining oil over a medium–high heat and stir in the cashews. Stir for about a minute, browning them all over and then stir in the chopped garlic, ginger and spring onions (scallions). Continue stirring for about a minute, then add the chilli flakes and (bell) pepper. Fry for about a minute to soften and then stir in the soy sauce, ketchup, honey and stock or water and chilli sauce. Bring to a simmer. This will help cook the pepper through and will also become the sauce.

Add the fried chicken and stir well to coat. The sauce should stick to the chicken strips. Season with salt and pepper to taste and sprinkle with toasted sesame seeds to serve. Dragon chicken is usually served just like this as a starter but you could make it into a more substantial meal by serving it over steamed rice.

PUNJABI CHICKEN SAMOSAS
SERVES 5–10

These are traditional Punjabi samosas. My favourite.

PREP TIME: 1 HOUR
COOKING TIME: 30 MINS

2 tbsp ghee
1 tsp cumin seeds
1 medium onion, very finely
    chopped
1 level tsp salt
2 tbsp garlic and ginger paste
3 green bird's eye chillies,
    finely chopped
1 medium tomato, finely diced
1 tsp Kashmiri chilli powder
    (more or less to taste)
1 tsp ground coriander
2 tbsp ground cumin
1 tsp garam masala
    (see page 161)
500g (1lb 2oz) minced (ground)
    chicken
3 tbsp fresh coriander (cilantro),
    finely chopped

FOR THE SAMOSA WRAPPERS

250g (2 cups) plain (all-purpose)
    flour, plus extra for dusting
1 tsp salt
1 tsp cumin or ajwain seeds
    (optional)
65ml (¼ cup) melted ghee or
    rapeseed (canola) oil
6 tbsp water

TO SERVE

Tamarind sauce
Green chilli and coriander
    chutney (see page 169)

Add the ghee to a pan over a medium–high heat. When the ghee has a glossy, shimmering appearance, stir in the cumin seeds and let them infuse for 30 seconds. Then add the onion and salt and fry for about 5 minutes or until soft and translucent. Stir in the garlic and ginger paste and chopped chillies and fry for another 30 seconds, then add the diced tomato and ground spices. Stir together.

Now add the chicken and 250ml (1 cup) of water. As the water comes to a simmer, break down the minced (ground) chicken until you see no lumps. Cover and cook for about 15 minutes, stirring occasionally. After 15 minutes, lift the lid and continue simmering until the water has evaporated and the chicken is beginning to brown. Add the chopped coriander (cilantro) and season with salt to taste, then transfer the filling to a plate to cool while you prepare the wrappers. Wipe your pan clean ready to fry the samosas.

Pour the flour into a bowl and add the salt, cumin/ajwain seeds and melted ghee or oil. Mix it together with your hands – it will become crumbly. Add the water slowly. You are aiming for a smooth, stiff dough, not soft. Once you have your dough ball formed, roughly 5–10 minutes of kneading, place it back in the bowl and cover with a damp cloth for 30 minutes.

Place the dough ball on a clean surface and roll it into a long cylinder shape. Slice it into 10 equal-sized pieces and then form each piece into firm, smaller balls. Place one ball on a lightly floured surface and roll it out until you have a circle that is just thinner than a tortilla. If you pick it up, you should be able to see your hand through it. Slice the circle in half into two semicircles. Keep the other dough balls covered so they don't dry out while you work.

Take a semicircle and join the corners to form a cone. Press the seam, so that the filling has no way of escaping, and fill the cone with a few tablespoons of the chicken. Press the top together into a triangle shape to close. Repeat with the remaining dough and filling.

To cook, slowly bring sufficient oil for deep-frying to a simmer over a medium heat. If you add a piece of dough, it should rise slowly to the top with only a few small bubbles around it. Add as many samosas as you can and fry for about 8 minutes, then turn up the heat to high. As the oil gets hotter, the samosas will begin to fry to a crispy golden brown. Each batch should take about 15 minutes but if you are cooking several batches, you will need to cool the oil down a little before adding each batch. Transfer the cooked samosas to a wire rack. No need to cover them – they will remain hot while you cook the remaining samosas.

CHICKEN SAMOSA CUPS
SERVES 5–10

As delicious as they are, you might not have the time or the will to make authentic Punjabi samosas (see page 21). You might not even want to go to the fuss of wrapping samosas using shop-bought samosa wrappers. Samosa cups are an ideal and easy-to-prepare substitute and make an excellent starter or snack with pre-dinner drinks. You could fill the samosa cups with whatever you like but here I have used the same filling as in my Punjabi samosas. To save you having to flip back and forth between pages, that recipe is here too. Although this recipe serves 5–10 people, if you have any leftover keema, you could always just bake up a couple of these samosa cups for a light snack.

PREP TIME: 15 MINS
COOKING TIME: 30 MINS

FOR THE KEEMA
2 tbsp rapeseed (canola) oil
    or ghee
1 tsp cumin seeds
1 medium onion, very finely
    chopped
1 level tsp salt
2 tbsp garlic and ginger paste
3 green bird's eye chillies,
    finely chopped
1 medium tomato, finely diced
1 tsp Kashmiri chilli powder
    (more or less to taste)
1 tsp ground coriander
2 tbsp ground cumin
1 tsp garam masala
    (see page 161)
500g (1lb 2oz) minced (ground)
    chicken
3 tbsp fresh coriander (cilantro),
    finely chopped

FOR THE SAMOSA CUPS
6 sheets of filo (phyllo) pastry
3 tbsp melted butter or ghee

TO SERVE
3 tbsp fresh coriander (cilantro),
    finely chopped

Add the oil or ghee to a pan over a medium–high heat. When the ghee or oil has a glossy, shimmering appearance, stir in the cumin seeds and let them infuse for 30 seconds. Then add the onion and salt and fry for about 5 minutes or until soft and translucent. Stir in the garlic and ginger paste and chopped chillies and fry for another 30 seconds, then add the diced tomato and ground spices. Stir together.

Now add the chicken and 250ml (1 cup) of water. As the water comes to a simmer, break down the minced (ground) chicken until you see no lumps. Cover and cook for about 15 minutes, stirring occasionally. After 15 minutes, lift the lid and continue simmering until the water has evaporated and the chicken is beginning to brown. Add the coriander (cilantro) and season with salt to taste, then transfer the filling to a plate to cool while you prepare the wrappers.

When you're ready to bake the samosa cups, preheat the oven to 180°C (350°F/Gas 4). Lay out your filo pastry sheets on a clean surface and brush each of the sheets with some of the melted butter or ghee. Stack the sheets neatly so that you have two stacks of three filo sheets. Use a cookie cutter or similar, which is around 10cm (4in) diameter, to cut your samosa cup rounds and cut as many as you can get from your filo sheets. I get about 12 but the number will depend on the size of your pastry sheets.

Brush a 12-hole cupcake tin lightly with some of the melted butter or ghee and fill each hole with one of the 3-ply circles. Fill each samosa with the chicken keema and bake in the oven for about 15 minutes or until the samosas look crisp and the meat is hot. Carefully transfer the samosas to a serving platter and garnish each with the fresh coriander (cilantro) and serve.

PANDAN CHICKEN
SERVES 4

This is a starter Caroline and I loved when we visited Kuala Lumpur. It's so simple and tastes amazing. Fresh pandan leaves can be a bit difficult to come by but they are available at most Southeast Asian shops in the freezer section and can also be purchased online. They really do make this chicken dish special, as they impart their flavour onto the chicken and also look great when served.

PREP TIME: 15 MINS
COOKING TIME: 30 MINS

500g (1lb 2oz) boneless chicken
  thighs, skinned and cut into
  10 large bite-sized pieces
10 fresh or frozen pandan leaves
4 tbsp rapeseed (canola) or
  peanut oil, for frying

FOR THE MARINADE

2 tbsp light soy sauce or tamari
2 tbsp sesame oil
2 tbsp oyster sauce
1 tbsp sugar
2 tbsp coriander (cilantro),
  roughly chopped
4 garlic cloves, roughly chopped
2.5cm (1in) piece of ginger,
  roughly chopped
½ tsp ground white pepper
½ tsp fish sauce

Place the marinade ingredients in a food processor or pestle and mortar and grind to a fine paste. Pour this marinade over the chicken in a mixing bowl and coat completely. Allow to marinate for at least 30 minutes or up to 3 hours.

Wash the pandan leaves under running water and cut into pieces that are large enough to wrap a couple of times around each chicken piece. Tie these pandan pieces around each piece of chicken. If you have trouble tying them, you could secure each pandan leaf with a toothpick.

Heat a pan over a medium high–heat and add the oil. Fry the pandan-wrapped chicken for about 10 minutes, turning regularly or until the chicken is cooked through.

Serve hot.

BAKED TANDOORI CHICKEN WINGS

SERVES 4–6

Have you ever tried to skin a chicken wing? It's not easy, so when you prepare these tandoori chicken wings, it's fine to leave the skin on. Although chicken skin isn't eaten often in Indian cuisine, you'll probably find these skin-on tandoori chicken wings some of the best on the planet! If you would like to eat lighter, you can find skinned chicken wings at most Indian or Pakistani grocers. You could also cook these in an air fryer or on your barbecue. If barbecuing, aim for about the same cooking temperature and cook over indirect heat (see page 127). Air fryers do vary, but I cook mine on high for about 20 minutes.

PREP TIME: 10 MINS
COOKING TIME: 30 MINS

1kg (2lb 2oz) chicken wings
1 tsp salt
1 tsp black pepper
Juice of 2 limes
3–5 green finger chillies
1 small bunch of coriander (cilantro), roughly chopped
4 tbsp Greek yoghurt
1 tbsp rapeseed (canola) oil
2 tbsp garlic and ginger paste
2 tsp ground coriander
2 tsp tandoori masala
2 tsp ground cumin
1 tsp chaat masala
1 tbsp Kashmiri chilli powder
1 tbsp smoked paprika or more chilli powder

TO SERVE
Lemon or lime wedges
Hot sauce or raita (see page 168)

Put the chicken wings in a large bowl and season generously with the salt and pepper. Squeeze the juice of one lime over all the wings and mix well to combine. You want that chicken coated with the salt, pepper and lime juice. Set aside while you prepare the marinade.

Pound the green chillies and coriander (cilantro) in a pestle and mortar until you have a paste. Add this paste to a large mixing bowl with the remaining ingredients, including the remaining lime juice, until smooth.

Pour this marinade over the chicken wings and again stir until the chicken is nicely coated with the marinade. You can go straight to cooking or place the chicken, covered, in the fridge for up to 24 hours. The longer, the better.

When ready to cook, place the chicken on a wire rack on a baking tray. Preheat the oven to 220°C (425°F/Gas 7). Place the chicken in the oven and cook for 30 minutes. Ovens do vary, so please be sure to check after about 20 minutes to see their progress. Turn the chicken wings over if you like a more equal roasting.

When cooked through, serve immediately with lemon or lime wedges and a good hot sauce or raita.

KARAHI
COOKING

Authentic and delicious, these karahi recipes are fun to prepare and get fantastic, restaurant-quality results. We're talking proper street-food karahi curries here!

Feel free to use less oil in these if you like, but if you want the real deal, that oil has to go in!

ABOUT THE KARAHI RECIPES

I must get asked for authentic karahi dishes more than any other recipes. If you've ever had a karahi curry prepared the way they do at street-food stalls in northern India and Pakistan, which you can find in the West too if you look, you'll know why these curries are so popular.

It's for this reason that I decided to feature all of the most popular street-food chicken karahis in this section, so that you have them all in one place to enjoy whenever you like.

I have developed these recipes for the home cook. The resulting curries will be just as authentic but prepared on a smaller scale. The following information will help you decide how you want to make these recipes.

WHAT EXACTLY IS A KARAHI CURRY?

You could say that any curry cooked in a karahi (a type of pan similar to a wok) is a karahi curry. There are curries, however, that are always cooked in karahis and are made just like the following karahi recipes. So when people in the know think of a karahi curry, they will be envisaging something like the recipes you will find in this chapter.

HOW MUCH OIL?

At large street-food stalls, the chicken is first deep-fried in a karahi full of oil. The majority of that oil is then poured out into another karahi to be used to cook more chicken. Depending on the vendor, anywhere from 125–250ml (½–1 cup) is left in the karahi to cook the curry. The karahi sauce is a smooth emulsion of that oil with other ingredients that are added. It really is good but even using the smaller amount of 125ml (½ cup), that's still 8 tablespoons of oil for a curry that serves four.

It is with the lesser amount of oil that I usually (but not always) prepare these curries. Once the oil does its job of creating one of the best curry sauces on the planet, the majority floats to the top. You could skim this oil off or serve it the traditional way, scooping up all that chicken, sauce and flavoured oil with hot chapattis or naans.

HOW THESE HOME COOK RECIPES DIFFER…

After cooking a few karahi curries exactly as I saw them being prepared, I decided to leave out the deep-frying. It is necessary for street-food vendors to have plenty of hot oil at the ready to cook with. If you are cooking a number of different karahi curries for friends, you might want to deep-fry so that you have a lot of hot oil ready. At home, you can just add 125ml (½ cup) oil and fry the chicken in that. If, when the chicken is cooked, you decide to use less oil, you can pour a little out, but I highly recommend using it all in the curry and then skimming the oil off at the end if you choose to do so.

What I have on offer for you here is karahi curries just as they should be. There are plenty of lighter curries in this book, so if the amount of oil looks like it's too much for you, I recommend making one of the others and perhaps saving the karahi recipes for days when you really want to splurge and treat yourself to something amazing. That said, if you must use less oil, you can still make these curries. You will need to add a little more water or stock to make the sauce. Your karahi curry will not be like the ones you get at street vendors and popular karahi restaurants, but it will still be good.

COOKING THE TOMATOES

At karahi food stalls, the karahi curries are cooked over an intense heat. Tomatoes are often added either halved or quartered. As the tomatoes cook in the hot oil, the skin comes off and this is fished out by the chef using tongs or a spatula. I have instructed you to do the same in the following recipes but there are a couple of other ways that might be more convenient for your style of cooking.

1. Bring some water to the boil and pour it over the tomatoes in a large bowl. Cover the bowl and allow it to sit for a few minutes. Then peel off the skin, which should come off easily, before adding the tomatoes to the karahi.
2. Use tinned (canned) chopped or whole tomatoes. The amount of tomatoes used in these recipes is approximately the equivalent of one to two 400g (14oz) cans.

ACHIEVING OPTIMUM FLAVOUR

Karahi curries are cooked over a high heat, making them the perfect curry for cooking over fire on your barbecue. As the sauce simmers, it will caramelize to the side of the pan. It is important to stir the curry often and be sure to scrape any caramelized sauce back in.

Most karahi chicken curries are cooked with chicken on the bone. If that doesn't appeal to you, you can use bite-sized pieces of chicken thighs or breasts. I used chicken off the bone in the Butter chicken karahi recipe on page 35.

ADVICE ABOUT KARAHI PANS AND SUBSTITUTES

You will have the best experience cooking these karahi curries if you use a large karahi and cook over a hot gas or charcoal flame. My karahi is round bottomed, 42cm (16.5in) in diameter, which makes it really easy to stir the ingredients around in the karahi. You could also use a large wok.

If you don't currently have either, you can use a large frying pan (skillet). It is a little more difficult and you will need to be a bit careful stirring the ingredients around or you might find that some of the sauce and ingredients end up on your stovetop.

During the photoshoot for this book, we used a variety of pans. Of course, cooking in the larger karahis and woks was the most fun and got the most accurate results but the smaller frying-pan cooks still produced fantastic and tasty dishes.

CHICKEN KARAHI WITH CHILLIES AND GARLIC
SERVES 4

This is the most basic of chicken karahis. Only a few easily sourced spices are added to the curry. The flavour comes from those spices with the fresh chillies, tomatoes, garlic, yoghurt and, of course, the chicken. The sauce is rich and out-of-this-world delicious, yet so simple. It's a great curry to try before moving on to the more extravagant versions that follow.

PREP TIME: 10 MINS
COOKING TIME: 30 MINS

125ml (½ cup) rapeseed
  (canola) oil
8 bullet chillies
10 garlic cloves, lightly smashed
1kg (2lb 2oz) chicken thighs on
  the bone, cut into 3 pieces
7 tomatoes, halved
1 tsp ground cumin
1 tsp ground coriander
1 tsp Kashmiri chilli powder
  (optional, more or less
  to taste)
2 tbsp garlic and ginger paste
250ml (1 cup) water
5 tbsp natural yoghurt, whisked
  until smooth
Salt, to taste

TO GARNISH (OPTIONAL)
4 tbsp coriander (cilantro),
  finely chopped
5cm (2in) piece of ginger, peeled
  and julienned

Heat the oil in a karahi or wok over a high heat. When bubbling hot, add the chillies and fry them for a few minutes or until blistered and darkened in places. Add the garlic and fry until it is beginning to turn golden brown. Using a slotted spoon, transfer the chillies and garlic to a plate and set aside.

Now add the chicken to the hot oil and fry for about 8 minutes, moving it around in the pan until white and just cooked through. Add the tomatoes and push them right down into the oil. Cover the pan and simmer over a low heat for about 7 minutes. Remove the lid and you will see that the skin of the tomatoes is peeling off. Remove the skins using your hands, or tongs which is much easier. If using tongs, give the tomatoes a good squeeze when you remove the skins to help break them down. If the skin is not coming off easily, just continue simmering and it will. Push the tomatoes right down into the chicken with the back of your spoon.

Add the ground spices and garlic and ginger paste. Then stir in the water and bring to a rolling simmer over a high heat, stirring often and hard to move everything around in the karahi. If the sauce is caramelizing to the sides of the karahi, scrape it back in for additional flavour.

Cover and simmer over a low heat for another 5–7 minutes, stirring from time to time. Lift the lid and stir in the yoghurt. Raise the heat to high and continue stirring vigorously to break that sauce down and thicken. Stir in the fried chillies and garlic and continue simmering and stirring until you are happy with the sauce consistency. Season with salt to taste and garnish with coriander (cilantro) and julienned ginger if you like.

BUTTER CHICKEN KARAHI
SERVES 4

Butter chicken, or Murgh makhani, is the hugely popular, mild curry from New Delhi. The curry sauce is slowly simmered before adding tandoori-style chicken, either on the bone or off. Any leftover marinade is also added to the sauce. There is, however, a karahi-style butter chicken which is not as well known outside India and Pakistan but is equally delicious. If you are a fan of butter chicken or chicken tikka masala, this is a karahi curry to put on your 'must try' list.

PREP TIME: 20 MINS
COOKING TIME: 20 MINS

125ml (½ cup) rapeseed (canola) oil or ghee

700g (1lb 9oz) boneless chicken thighs, skinned and cut into small bite-sized pieces

1 tsp salt

1 tsp freshly ground black pepper

2 tsp ground cumin

2 tsp ground coriander

1 tsp ground turmeric

1 tsp Kashmiri chilli powder

5 medium tomatoes, halved

75g (¼ cup) natural yoghurt, whisked until creamy smooth

5 tbsp single (light) cream

2 tbsp butter

1 tsp kasoori methi (dried fenugreek leaves)

TO SERVE

5cm (2in) piece of ginger, peeled and julienned

3 tbsp coriander (cilantro), finely chopped

2 green finger chillies, thinly sliced (if you like a bit of spice)

Heat the oil or ghee in a karahi or wok over a high heat. Add the diced chicken and fry for about 4 minutes or until white on the exterior and almost cooked through. Season with the salt and pepper and add the ground spices. Stir this all together to coat the chicken. Add the tomatoes and push them down into the simmering sauce. Reduce the heat to low, cover the pan and cook for 5–7 minutes, stirring occasionally.

Lift the lid. The skin from the tomatoes should be coming off; remove this with tongs or your hands. It should come off easily but if it doesn't, raise the heat again to high and simmer until the skin can be easily removed. If you are using tongs, give the tomatoes a good squeeze as you remove the skins. This will help them break down into the sauce. Push the peeled tomatoes down into the sauce, smashing them as you do. Then add the yoghurt and stir it into the sauce.

Reduce the heat to low again, cover the pan and cook for about 5 minutes. Stir from time to time, pushing the tomatoes down and breaking them apart. After 5 minutes, remove the lid and turn up the heat to high. Add the cream and stir constantly, scraping any sauce that begins to caramelize on the side of the pan back in for additional flavour. Keep stirring. You want the tomatoes, cream and yoghurt to emulsify with the oil into a smooth sauce.

When you are happy with your sauce, add the butter and let it begin to melt into the sauce, while continuing to stir. Add the kasoori methi by rubbing the leaves between your fingers. Although this is not butter chicken like you might have tried before, it should look like it. Keep stirring until the sauce comes together and looks like butter chicken!

Try the curry and add more salt and pepper to taste if you like. Top with the julienned ginger and coriander (cilantro). If you like a bit of spice, top with thinly sliced chillies too.

WHITE CHICKEN KARAHI (KORMA)
SERVES 4

White chicken karahi is the closest I found to the British curry house korma while in northern India. I'm sure there are others but this one is perfect if you are serving people who don't like spicy curries. The banana chillies are quite mild and added more for colour. You could leave them out if you don't want any spicy flavours at all.

PREP TIME: 15 MINS
COOKING TIME: 15 MINS

375ml (1½ cups) water
125ml (1 cup) rapeseed (canola) oil
1 tbsp ghee
1kg (2lb 2oz) chicken thighs on the bone, cut in half and skinned
250ml (1 cup) natural yoghurt
3 tbsp milk
½ tsp ground white pepper
2 tsp garam masala (see page 161)
1 tsp ground cumin
1 tsp ground coriander
1 tbsp coconut milk powder (optional) ★
3 banana chillies, halved lengthwise down the centre
125ml (½ cup) single (light) cream
5cm (2in) piece of ginger, peeled and julienned
3 tbsp coriander (cilantro), finely chopped
1 lime, sliced into about 6 thin rounds
Salt, to taste

Bring the water to the boil in a karahi or wok and add the oil, ghee and chicken. Simmer over a high heat, stirring often until almost all of the liquid has evaporated and the chicken is white and cooked through. While the chicken is cooking, whisk the yoghurt and milk together so they are ready to add.

Once the chicken is cooked through and only a little liquid is left in the karahi, stir in the ground spices, followed by the coconut milk powder. Then stir in the whisked yoghurt so that it coats the chicken.

Add the sliced chillies. Yoghurt tends to curdle, so really get in there and move the sauce around to keep it smooth. If your yoghurt does curdle, it isn't a big problem as the lumps should eventually emulsify into the smooth white sauce. Just keep stirring vigorously.

Continue simmering to thicken the yoghurt sauce. The sauce will become quite thick, clinging to the meat after a few minutes. When it does, pour in the cream and continue simmering and stirring it all together in the hot karahi.

Once you have a sauce consistency you are happy with, season with salt to taste and garnish with the julienned ginger, coriander (cilantro) and lime slices.

★ NOTE

Coconut milk powder is not the same as coconut flour. Coconut flour is made from the dried, ground meat of the coconut. Coconut milk powder is made from the coconut milk and is much finer. It is available at Indian grocers and online. If you have trouble sourcing it, you could simply add a couple of tablespoons of thick coconut milk.

CHICKEN KEEMA KARAHI
SERVES 4

I decided to give you this recipe the way I saw it prepared in New Delhi. The chicken keema wasn't finely minced (ground) but finely chopped instead. It was also first deep-fried in oil. The majority of the oil is then poured away for later use but if you really don't want to use that much oil, go ahead and add just enough to fry the chicken: 125ml (1 cup) should do the job but feel free to use even less. This recipe demonstrates how much oil is used and how it is used at many street vendors but, as mentioned on page 30, how much oil you actually add is down to you.

PREP TIME: 10 MINS
COOKING TIME: 20 MINS

500ml (2 cups) rapeseed (canola) oil
700g (1lb 9oz) skinless chicken thighs, finely minced (ground) with a sharp knife
2 tbsp garlic and ginger paste
2–4 green bird's eye chillies, thinly sliced
1 tsp Kashmiri chilli powder
1 tsp ground cumin
1 tsp ground coriander
½ tsp ground turmeric
5–6 tomatoes, halved
250ml (1 cup) chicken stock or water
10 green bullet chillies, roughly chopped
Salt and pepper, to taste

TO GARNISH
5cm (2in) piece of ginger, peeled and julienned
3 tbsp coriander (cilantro), finely chopped

Heat the oil in a large karahi or wok over a medium–high heat. When visibly hot and you hear a faint hissing sound, add the finely minced (ground) chicken and move it all around in the hot oil. Fry for about 5 minutes or until cooked through and just beginning to get crispy in places. Pour out all but about 125ml (½ cup) of the oil. You can discard the oil or strain and use it in another dish (see Note).

Stir the garlic and ginger paste into the chicken and continue frying and stirring for about a minute. Add the bird's eye chillies and ground spices and stir well to combine. Then add the halved tomatoes and chicken stock or water. Bring to a simmer, then cover the pan to continue simmering for about 5 minutes.

Take the lid off the pan and continue cooking. As the sauce simmers and thickens, the tomato skins will begin to come off. Fish them out with your hands, or tongs which is easier. If using tongs, give the tomatoes a good squeeze as you remove the skins. This will help them fall apart into the sauce. As the curry continues to cook, the remaining oil will begin to rise to the top. You could skim this off the top or leave it in, which is more authentic and delicious too.

Stir in the bullet chillies and let them cook in the hot keema for a couple of minutes. They should look fresh and not completely cooked. Season with salt and pepper to taste and then garnish with the julienned ginger and coriander (cilantro) to serve.

NOTE
I never throw away leftover cooking oil and tend to reuse it at least once if not three times. I do, however, cook pretty much every day. You can reuse oil after frying chicken by filtering out the debris and allowing it to cool completely before storing it in an airtight container. The oil's reusability depends on factors like oil type, frying temperature and food variety. Before reuse, you could also do a fry test. If the oil smells off, looks dark or has a rancid flavour, discard it.

It is important to prioritize food safety and quality and that information is beyond the scope of this cookbook. If the oil shows signs of going off, replace it with fresh oil for optimal frying results.

CHICKEN JALFREZI KARAHI
SERVES 4

Traditionally, jalfrezis were made with leftover cooked meat. In this recipe, we're going to throw that all out the window and cook the meat in the karahi from raw. In the popular karahi version of this recipe, the chicken would be deep-fried as it is in the keema and bhuna recipes in this chapter. I just wanted to demonstrate that you can really mix things up and still come up with an amazing curry that's far closer to the jalfrezis being consumed by the staff at the back of restaurants than what is served at the front to customers. This and the other karahi curries in this chapter are heavy in oil and they benefit from it too. Feel free to use less if you like, but you might need to add a little stock or water for the sauce.

PREP TIME: 15 MINS
COOKING TIME: 25 MINS

125ml (½ cup) rapeseed (canola) oil
1 tsp black mustard seeds
1 tsp cumin seeds
2 large onions, very thinly sliced
6 tomatoes, halved
3–4 green bird's eye chillies, thinly sliced (or to taste)
1kg (2lb 2oz) chicken thighs, skin removed, on the bone and cut in half
1 tsp ground cumin
1 tsp ground coriander
½ tsp ground turmeric
1 tbsp garam masala (see page 161)
1–2 tsp Kashmiri chilli powder
1 green (bell) pepper, seeded and cut into bite-sized pieces
1 yellow (bell) pepper, seeded and cut into bite-sized pieces
1 medium red onion, quartered and broken into petals
Salt, to taste

TO GARNISH

5cm (2in) piece of ginger, peeled and julienned
5 tbsp coriander (cilantro), finely chopped

Heat the oil in a large karahi or wok over a high heat. Add the mustard seeds and, when they begin to crackle in the hot oil, add the cumin seeds, followed immediately by the sliced onions. Fry the onions for about 7 minutes, stirring often until they are soft and turning a light golden brown. Add the halved tomatoes and sliced chillies and cover the pan. Reduce the heat to low and simmer gently for 7 minutes.

Lift the lid. You will find that the skin from the tomatoes is beginning to peel off. Peel the skin and remove it when it is easy to do so. You could use tongs to do this as it's easier than using your hands. You might need to cook a little longer to remove all the skin, smashing the tomatoes into the onions as you do so.

Add about 1 teaspoon of salt and stir it in. Then add the chicken and all the ground spices and stir well to coat. Cover the pan and continue cooking over a low–medium heat for about 8 minutes. Lift the lid again and stir in the (bell) peppers and red onion. Continue simmering over a medium–high heat until the sauce has reduced down to your liking and the (bell) peppers and onion are just cooked through. Season with salt to taste and garnish with the julienned ginger and chopped coriander (cilantro).

CHICKEN BHUNA KARAHI
SERVES 4

Bhuna curries are curry house favourites but at most they are prepared with a base curry sauce. In this recipe, we're going more authentic and, believe me, the end result is amazing! This is a curry with a thick sauce, perfect for picking up with fresh naans or chapattis. I really hope you prepare the spice masala as described below, but if you're in a rush, you could substitute 2 tablespoons of a good-quality garam masala. This is a spicy one! If concerned about the heat, add less chilli powder or substitute it for paprika, which will give the curry a nice red colour.

PREP TIME: 10 MINS
COOKING TIME: 30 MINS

1 x 1.5kg (3lb 5oz) whole chicken, skin removed and cut into 10 pieces
2–3 tsp chilli powder
1 tsp ground turmeric
1 tsp salt
3 tbsp lime or lemon juice

FOR THE CURRY
80ml (⅓ cup) rapeseed (canola) oil
3 large red onions, very finely chopped
2 tbsp garlic and ginger paste
6 tomatoes, halved
5 green finger chillies, slit lengthwise down the middle
2 tsp Kashmiri chilli powder or paprika
½ tsp ground turmeric
1 tsp kasoori methi (dried fenugreek leaves)
4 tbsp coriander (cilantro), finely chopped
1 lemon, sliced
Salt and pepper, to taste

FOR THE BHUNA SPICE BLEND
1 tbsp cumin seeds
1 tbsp coriander seeds
1 tbsp black peppercorns
1 star anise
4 black cardamom pods, seeds only
3 cloves
5cm (2in) cinnamon stick
1 tsp fennel seeds

Put all of the bhuna spice blend ingredients in a dry frying pan (skillet) and toast them over a medium–high heat until warm to the touch and fragrant but not yet smoking. This should take about 3 minutes. If your spices begin to smoke, get them off the heat. Pour onto a plate to cool a little and then grind to a fine powder using a spice grinder or pestle and mortar. Set aside.

Pour the chicken pieces into a mixing bowl and sprinkle the chilli powder, turmeric, salt and lime or lemon juice over the top. Mix well with your hands or a spoon to coat. Set aside to marinate for about 30 minutes, or just start cooking. The longer marination time will help intensify the flavours.

When ready to cook, heat the oil in a karahi or wok over a high heat and, when visibly hot, add the finely chopped onions. Fry for about 7 minutes, stirring often, or until the onions are beginning to turn a light golden brown. Stir in the garlic and ginger paste and fry for a further 30 seconds. Reduce the heat to medium and add the halved tomatoes and chillies and the marinated chicken. Stir well to combine and continue stirring for a couple of minutes.

At this time, your pan might be looking a bit dry. That is what you are looking for as bhunas are drier curries. Reduce the heat to low, cover the pan and simmer gently for 8 minutes. Lift the lid; the skin will have started to come off the tomatoes. Using tongs or your hands, remove the tomato skins. If using tongs, you can squeeze the tomatoes, which will assist and speed up the cooking. Give it another good stir, then stir in the bhuna spice blend, the chilli powder and turmeric. The onions, chicken and tomatoes will have released liquid into the sauce and your bhuna will look nowhere near as dry as earlier. Cover the pan again and continue cooking over a low heat for another 5–6 minutes.

Lift the lid again and your bhuna will be much more liquidy. Turn up the heat to medium–high and cook for a further 7–10 minutes to thicken the sauce. When the sauce consistency is to your liking, try the curry and add salt and pepper to taste. Add the kasoori methi (dried fenugreek leaves) by rubbing it between your fingers and garnish with coriander (cilantro) and sliced lemon to serve.

CHICKEN CHOLE KARAHI
SERVES 4–6

When I make this at home, I always use dried chickpeas, which I soak and then cook until soft. Not only is the texture of the chickpeas nicer, but you also get to add the cooking liquid to this amazing curry instead of just water. This curry is filling and although it is great served over rice or with naans, it can also be served on its own.

PREP TIME: 15 MINS, PLUS SOAKING
COOKING TIME: UP TO 2 HOURS

500g (1lb 2oz) dried chickpeas, soaked in water overnight, or 4 x 400g (14oz) tins (cans) chickpeas (garbanzo beans)
125ml (½ cup) ghee
1 tsp black peppercorns
6 green cardamom pods, lightly crushed
5cm (2in) cinnamon stick
1 tbsp cumin seeds
3 cloves
2 medium red onions, finely chopped
2 tbsp garlic and ginger paste
3 medium tomatoes, halved
1 tbsp red chilli flakes
2 tsp ground cumin
1 tbsp ground coriander
½ tsp ground turmeric
600g (1lb 5oz) chicken thighs, on the bone and each cut into 3 pieces
125ml (½ cup) chicken stock or water (optional)
Salt and pepper, to taste

TO GARNISH
3 tbsp coriander (cilantro), finely chopped
5cm (2in) piece of ginger, peeled and julienned
1–2 lemons, quartered

If using dried chickpeas, cook them first. Pour the washed and soaked chickpeas into a large saucepan and cover completely with water. Bring to a simmer over a medium–high heat and cook for about 1 hour 10 minutes or until the chickpeas are soft enough to smash between your fingers. Strain but retain the cooking liquid for later.

Place roughly half of the cooked chickpeas in a food processor and blend to a thick paste. If using tinned (canned) chickpeas, do the same. Set aside.

Put a karahi or wok over a medium–high heat and melt the ghee. Then add the black peppercorns, cardamom pods, cinnamon stick, cumin seeds and cloves and let their flavours infuse into the ghee for about 40 seconds. Stir in the chopped onions and continue frying for about 8 minutes or until the onions are turning a light golden brown. Stir in the garlic and ginger paste.

Add the tomatoes and cover the pan. Let this all simmer for 5–7 minutes over a low heat. Lift the lid and give it all a good stir. The skins of the tomatoes will be peeling off. If not, simmer a little longer and they will. Remove the skins using your hands or tongs and discard. If using tongs, give the tomatoes a good squeeze as you remove the skins to help break them apart into the sauce. Stir in the chilli flakes, cumin, coriander and turmeric. Add the chicken and stir it right into the sauce. Continue to cook until the chicken is cooked through, stirring often. Then add the remaining whole or tinned (canned) chickpeas with about 125ml (½ cup) of the cooking liquid, or the chicken stock or water. Cover the pan and simmer over a low heat for 5 minutes. Give it all a good stir and add the blended chickpeas.

The curry will look a bit dry, so go ahead and add more of the cooking liquid from the chickpeas, stock or water. I usually add about 250ml (1 cup). Cover again and simmer over a low heat for 10 minutes. The ghee will rise to the top and the flavour of it all will be incredible. If you prefer more liquid, just add it until you are happy with the consistency. Season with salt and freshly ground black pepper to taste and garnish with chopped coriander (cilantro) and/or julienned ginger. If you like, serve with lemon wedges that can be squeezed over the curry at the table.

CHICKEN SAAG KARAHI

SERVES 4

This has to be my favourite chicken saag recipe. There are quite a few ingredients but it's worth gathering them all together and cooking this delicious and hugely popular karahi curry. Although great over rice, I like to serve this with naans or parathas. The sauce is thick and perfect for picking up with the hot breads.

PREP TIME: 15 MINS
COOKING TIME: 35 MINS

240g (9oz) spinach leaves, chopped
2 bunches (approx. 150g/5½oz) of mustard leaves, chopped
½ bunch (approx. 80g/3oz) of fresh fenugreek leaves, chopped
125ml (½ cup) rapeseed (canola) oil
1 tsp cumin seeds
2 brown onions, sliced paper thin
2 tbsp garlic and ginger paste
5 tomatoes, halved
1 tbsp Kashmiri chilli powder
2 tsp ground coriander
1½ tsp ground cumin
½ tsp ground turmeric
1 tbsp natural yoghurt
1kg (2lb 2oz) chicken thighs, skin removed, on the bone and cut in half
70ml (¼ cup) water
2 tsp garam masala (see page 161)
Salt, to taste

Start by preparing the saag sauce. Wash the spinach, mustard and fenugreek leaves thoroughly under cold running water to remove any grit that might be on them. Bring a pot of water to the boil and add the greens. Simmer for 30 seconds and then strain. Allow to cool a little, then place the blanched greens in a food processor and blend to a thick paste. You can use a little water to assist blending if needed. Set aside.

Now heat the oil over a medium–high heat in a karahi or wok and, when you can see gentle ripples or waves on the surface of the oil, stir in the cumin seeds. Allow the cumin to infuse into the hot oil for about 30 seconds and then stir in the chopped onions and 1 teaspoon of salt. Fry for about 10 minutes, stirring often until the onions are a light golden brown. Add the garlic and ginger paste and stir it into the fried onions for about 30 seconds.

Add the tomatoes and cover the pan. Allow to simmer over a low heat for 5–7 minutes, stirring occasionally. After about 5 minutes, the tomato skins will begin to come off. Remove the skin with your hands or tongs and smash the tomatoes down into the sauce.

The sauce will be quite broken down now but you will still see pieces of the tomato. Stir in the chilli powder, coriander, cumin and turmeric followed by the yoghurt. Add the chicken and stir it right into the sauce to coat. Cover the pan again and simmer over a medium heat for 5–7 minutes, stirring from time to time.

The chicken should now be almost cooked through and the sauce will be a deep red colour. Add the blended spinach mixture and stir it right in. Pour in the water and the garam masala and cover the pan again. Simmer, covered, over a low heat for 15 minutes, stirring from time to time. This is normally a dry curry but you could add a little water to thin it out if you prefer.

As the curry simmers, the oil will rise to the top. This is a good indication that the curry is ready to serve. Try it and season with salt to taste.

BLACK PEPPER CHICKEN KARAHI
SERVES 4

All of the karahi recipes featured in this book were most likely being prepared long before chillies were introduced to the Indian subcontinent. This recipe gets its spiciness from freshly ground black pepper. It's so good just as it is, though I do like to garnish it with fresh coriander (cilantro) and thinly sliced green chillies for colour.

PREP TIME: 15 MINS
COOKING TIME: 20 MINS

125ml rapeseed (canola) oil
1kg (2lb 2oz) chicken thighs,
    skinned and each one cut
    into 3 pieces
5 medium tomatoes, halved
2 tbsp garlic and ginger paste
2 tsp freshly ground black
    pepper
250ml (1 cup) natural yoghurt,
    whisked
2 tsp ground cumin
2 tsp ground coriander
Salt and pepper, to taste

TO GARNISH (OPTIONAL)

4 tbsp coriander (cilantro),
    finely chopped
3–4 green finger chillies,
    thinly sliced

Heat the oil in a karahi or wok over a high heat. Add the chicken and 1 teaspoon of salt and fry for about 5 minutes or until white on the exterior and nearly cooked through. Add the halved tomatoes and stir them into the chicken. Cover the pan and cook over a medium heat for 5–7 minutes, lifting the lid from time to time to stir.

Remove the lid and you will see that the tomato skins are coming free from the tomatoes. Using your hands, or tongs which is easier, remove the skins and discard. If the skins are not coming off easily, just simmer and stir a bit longer and they will. If using tongs, give the tomatoes a good squeeze, which will help break them down into the sauce. Stir in the garlic and ginger paste and the freshly ground black pepper and stir well to combine. Then add the yoghurt and again stir well so that the chicken is completely coated.

Turn up the heat to high and stir, stir, stir! If the sauce is caramelizing on the sides of the pan, scrape it back into the sauce. Now add the cumin and coriander and stir into the sauce as well. Give it all another good stir, scraping the sides of the karahi as you do, then reduce the heat to low and cover the pan. Simmer, covered, for another 5 minutes.

When you lift the lid, the oil will have risen to the top. This is a good indication that the curry is ready to serve. Try it and add more salt and freshly ground black pepper to taste. Garnish with chopped coriander (cilantro) and thinly sliced chillies if you like.

CHICKEN NAMKEEN KARAHI
SERVES 4

Chicken namkeen is special in that the chicken and sauce are cooked with rendered chicken fat, which adds a rich and not-to-be-missed flavour. In my book *The Curry Guy Bible*, I featured a recipe for this hugely popular karahi curry which was cooked the same way but with tinned (canned) tomatoes and a few other changes for authenticity. I decided to include this recipe so that you have all the most popular karahi curries in one book, but this is a drier version. The thick sauce coats and flavours the meat and it's amazing picking up a piece with a naan or chapatti and dipping it back into that delicious sauce. I have included a recipe for rendered chicken fat below this recipe. You could also purchase schmaltz (rendered chicken fat) online and at speciality grocers. I recommend making your own though, because the chicken skin you get as a by-product is better than pork crackling!

PREP TIME: 20 MINS
COOKING TIME: 20 MINS

250ml (1 cup) rendered chicken fat
1 x 1.5kg (3lb 5oz) whole chicken, skin removed and cut into about 20 pieces
6 tomatoes, halved
6 (or more) green bird's eye chillies, slit lengthwise down the centre
1 tsp black pepper
Salt, to taste
5cm (2in) piece of ginger, peeled and julienned, to garnish

Heat a large karahi or wok over a high heat and pour in the rendered chicken fat. Add the chicken and fry until cooked through. This should take about 5–8 minutes. Stir regularly so that it cooks evenly.

Once cooked, pour out all but about 125ml (½ cup) of the fat. This can be frozen and used another time. Add the tomatoes, reduce the heat to low and cover the pan. Simmer lightly for 5–7 minutes, stirring occasionally.

Lift the lid and the tomato skins should be peeling off. Remove the skins with tongs or your hands. The skin should come off easily but if not, raise the heat to high and continue simmering. It will eventually peel off and the tomatoes will break down into the sauce.

Continue simmering and scraping any sauce that caramelizes to the sides of the pan back in. This is quite a thick sauce and it should literally cling to the meat.

When you are happy with the sauce consistency, stir in the chillies and black pepper. Turn off the heat and add salt to taste. Garnish with the julienned ginger.

HOW TO RENDER CHICKEN FAT

Rendering your own chicken fat is easy: purchase two 1.5kg (3lb 5oz) chickens, remove the fat and the skin from the carcasses and cut into small 2.5cm (1in) pieces. Fry the fat and skin in a non-stick pan over a medium heat for 5 minutes. This will release some fat. Cover the skin and fat with 500ml (2 cups) of water and simmer, covered, for 1 hour. Lift the lid and turn the crispy fat over and fry the other side for a further 20 minutes, uncovered. By now, all the water will have evaporated and you will be left with enough fat for this curry. Use one of the chickens for the curry and use the other for another recipe.

CHICKEN CURRIES, STEWS AND SAUCE-BASED DISHES

Here you'll find many popular, deliciously spiced curries, stews and sauce-based dishes from around the Indian subcontinent and Southeast Asia.

Whether you're looking for a traditional spicy korma from northern India or you just want to enjoy a light but satisfying chicken soup from Vietnam or Indonesia, you'll find a great selection in this chapter.

JEERA (CUMIN) CHICKEN CURRY

SERVES 4

Cumin is the second most popular spice in the world, second only to black pepper. I love it, and this jeera chicken is a firm favourite around our house. If you're a fan of cumin too, you are going to want to make this soon.

PREP TIME: 10 MINS
COOKING TIME: 30 MINS

4 tbsp cumin seeds
70ml (¼ cup) rapeseed
   (canola) oil
1 onion, thinly sliced
1 generous tbsp garlic and
   ginger paste
2 green bird's eye chillies,
   finely chopped
½ tsp ground turmeric
½ tsp Kashmiri chilli powder
1 tbsp garam masala
   (see page 161)
1 tsp ground coriander
700g (1lb 9oz) skinless chicken
   thighs, cut into bite-sized
   pieces
125ml (½ cup) water
2–3 generous tbsp natural
   yoghurt
Salt, to taste
3 tbsp coriander (cilantro),
   finely chopped (optional),
   to garnish

Toast 2 tablespoons of the cumin seeds in a dry frying pan (skillet) over a medium heat until fragrant and warm to the touch. Be careful not to burn the cumin or it will become bitter. Grind the cumin into a powder in a mortar or spice grinder and set aside.

Heat the oil in a large pan or wok over a medium–high heat. When the oil begins to shimmer, add the sliced onion and fry for about 10 minutes until golden brown in colour but not burnt. With a slotted spoon, transfer the fried onion to a paper towel to soak up excess oil. You only need 2 tablespoons of oil for the curry. If you want, you can transfer the rest to a jar to use as onion-seasoned oil in other recipes.

Reduce the heat to medium and add the remaining 2 tablespoons of cumin seeds to the oil and fry for about 30 seconds to infuse their flavour into the oil. Stir in the garlic and ginger paste and fry for about 30 seconds, just to cook off the rawness. Add the chopped chillies and the turmeric, chilli powder, garam masala, ground coriander and the toasted ground cumin and stir well to combine.

Now add the chicken and fry for about 5 minutes to brown in the oil and spice mixture. Add a couple of tablespoons of the water so that the spices don't burn. Return the fried onion and the remaining water to the pan and stir well. Cover the pan and simmer for another 5–10 minutes or until the chicken is cooked through.

Stir in the yoghurt, 1 tablespoon at a time, and continue cooking until you are happy with the sauce consistency. You can always add more yoghurt or water if you prefer more sauce. Season with salt to taste and garnish with fresh coriander (cilantro) to serve.

AYAM RICA RICA
SERVES 4

Ayam rica rica is a spicy chicken dish from the North Sulawesi region of Indonesia. It is known for its bold and fiery flavours. If you aren't a fan of really spicy curries, use fewer red bird's eye chillies. Spur chillies aren't very spicy and give the dish its characteristic red glow. Some chefs in Indonesia use fewer chillies to please the spice-wary tourists and add one or two chopped tomatoes. I tend to leave the tomato out and go with the spicy chillies instead, but that is all up to you.

PREP TIME: 15 MINS
COOKING TIME: 25 MINS

3 tbsp rapeseed (canola) oil
3 shallots (approx. 75g/2½oz), thinly sliced
1 pandan leaf, tied in a knot (optional)
2 lemongrass stalks, lightly smashed
1kg (2lb 2oz) bone-in or boneless chicken thighs, skinned and cut in half
70ml (¼ cup) water or chicken stock
4 makrut lime leaves, stalks removed and torn in a few places
Salt, to taste
1 large lemon or 2 limes, cut into wedges, to serve

FOR THE PASTE

5 large shallots (approx. 100g/ 3½oz), roughly chopped
8 garlic cloves, smashed
2.5cm (1in) piece of ginger, roughly chopped
2.5cm (1in) piece of galangal, roughly chopped
10 red spur chillies, roughly chopped
5 red bird's eye chillies, roughly chopped (or to taste)

Start by placing all the paste ingredients in a blender and blend them to a smooth paste. You could add a couple of drops of water if needed to assist with the blending. Set aside.

Heat the oil in a large frying pan (skillet) over a medium–high heat and stir in the sliced shallots, knotted pandan leaf, if using, and the bruised lemongrass stalks. Fry for about 5 minutes, stirring often, until the shallots are just starting to turn a light brown. Stir in the blended paste and fry for a further 3 minutes. As it fries, the oil will begin to separate and the paste will thicken a little, which is a good sign that it's time to add your chicken.

Add the chicken and stir well so that it is all nicely coated with the paste. Then add the water or chicken stock, cover the pan and simmer over a medium heat for 15 minutes.

After 15 minutes, lift the lid and stir in the lime leaves. Season with salt to taste and serve hot over white rice, with the lime wedges to squeeze over at the table.

NOTE

You might like to add some passata or blended tomatoes either for colour or to cool it down some if you feel it is too spicy. You can do this but only add a couple of tablespoons at a time. Taste as you go and add it to taste.

SOTO AYAM
SERVES 4

You can't go to Indonesia without running into this soup. This was my breakfast most mornings while there, but it's much more common to have this for lunch or dinner in the West. Traditionally, this is a fragrant and delicious chicken soup that isn't spicy. I always asked for chopped chillies with mine to turn up the heat a bit, but you can leave the chillies out if you like. You can use water instead of chicken stock for this recipe, as the chicken produces a good stock anyway, but you will get a soup with more depth of flavour using chicken stock.

PREP TIME: 15 MINS
COOKING TIME: 1 HOUR

2 tbsp rapeseed (canola) or
    peanut oil
2 lemongrass stalks, tough
    outer leaves removed,
    lightly crushed
6 makrut lime leaves
1.5 litres (6 cups) chicken stock
    or water
1 tsp Asian chicken powder
    (contains MSG and
    is optional)
8 large chicken thighs on the
    bone, skin removed
100g (3½oz) dried rice vermicelli
100g (3½oz) shredded
    green cabbage
1 small bunch of coriander
    (cilantro), roughly chopped
2 tomatoes, quartered
4 hard-boiled eggs, halved
    (optional)
2 spring onions (scallions),
    thinly sliced into rings
1 tsp sugar (or to taste)
4 red finger chillies or bird's eye
    chillies, thinly sliced into
    rings (optional)
Salt, to taste
2 limes, quartered, to serve

FOR THE PASTE
8 garlic cloves, smashed
2.5cm (1 inch) piece of ginger,
    roughly chopped
2 macadamia or candle nuts,
    lightly smashed (optional
    for thickening)
5 medium shallots (approx.
    100g/3½oz), roughly chopped
½ tsp ground turmeric

Prepare the paste by placing the ingredients in a blender and blending to a smooth, pourable paste. Set aside. This can be done a day or so ahead of cooking if more convenient.

When ready to cook, heat the oil over a medium–high heat in a saucepan that is large enough to hold all the ingredients. Stir in the prepared paste and fry for about 3 minutes to cook out the raw flavour. Then add the crushed lemongrass and the lime leaves. Fry for a further minute and then add the chicken stock or water and the Asian chicken powder, if using. Add the chicken to the stock and bring to a simmer. Then reduce the heat to medium and simmer, covered, for 45 minutes.

After 45 minutes, lift the lid and remove the chicken with a slotted spoon. Transfer the chicken to a plate and set aside. Keep warm. Continue simmering the soup for another 15 minutes.

While the soup is simmering, you can finish up this dish. Pour boiling water over the rice vermicelli noodles and let them sit in the water until cooked. This should only take a couple of minutes. Strain and divide between four soup bowls. Top each bowl with some chicken, shredded cabbage, coriander (cilantro), a couple of tomato wedges, two halves of egg, if using, and the spring onions (scallions). Taste the stock and add a little sugar if you prefer a sweeter flavour and also add salt to taste.

Add a couple of ladles of the stock to each bowl and serve hot with a side of chopped chillies, if you like, and some lime wedges for squeezing over.

CHICKEN PALLIPALAYAM
SERVES 4

Chicken pallipalayam is a famous Tamil Nadu recipe. The chicken is first browned and charred in the pan and no water is added. This is a dry curry and the only liquid required is the liquid from the onions, garlic and chicken. A good heavy-bottomed pan is best for this cooking method as the chicken really needs to cook long and slow for optimum flavour. The lightly charred juicy chicken, together with the crunchy coconut pieces, are what makes this curry unique and out-of-this-world delicious. That and adding the fresh curry leaves at the end, which is quite common in southern India, both for their flavour and as a nice garnish.

PREP TIME: 15 MINS
COOKING TIME: 1 HOUR
10 MINS

3 tbsp coconut oil
10 dried Kashmiri chillies,
   chopped (seeded for a
   milder curry)
1 small red onion, finely
   chopped
½ tsp ground turmeric
½ tsp salt
1 x 1kg (2lb 2oz) whole chicken,
   skinned and cut into about
   12 pieces
¼ fresh or frozen coconut,
   cut into thin slices or
   finely chopped
20 fresh curry leaves, thoroughly
   washed
Salt and pepper, to taste

FOR THE PASTE
8 large shallots (approx. 200g/
   1 cup), roughly chopped
8 garlic cloves
10 curry leaves

Place all the paste ingredients in a food processor or spice grinder and grind to a coarse paste. Do not add water. This paste should not be wet and smooth but rather very finely chopped. You could also do this with a sharp knife if you like. Set aside.

When ready to cook the curry, heat the oil in a large pan or wok over a medium–high heat and stir in the chopped dried chillies. Stir in the chopped onion and fry for about 8 minutes or until it turns golden brown, soft and translucent. Then stir in the prepared garlic and shallot paste and continue frying and stirring for another 3 minutes.

Stir in the ground turmeric and salt, followed by the chicken pieces and mix well. Cover the pan, turn down the heat to low and cook for about 15 minutes. Do not add any water as the onions and chicken will release enough for this dish.

After 15 minutes, give it all a good stir. You will notice that there is now water from the chicken and onion in the pan. If not, then you have been cooking on too high a heat, so tone it down a little! Add a drop of water or stock if you must. Cover the pan again and continue simmering over a low heat for another 20–30 minutes. Cooking the chicken like this will begin to roast the chicken on the underside.

After 20–30 minutes, when the chicken is looking lightly brown and cooked through, stir in the coconut, cover the pan again and cook for a further 5 minutes. Add the fresh curry leaves and turn off the heat. Serve with hot buttered white rice or chapattis.

SOUTH INDIAN CHICKEN DRUMSTICK CURRY

SERVES 4

Of course you could use other cuts of chicken for this popular curry but it is traditionally made with drumsticks. Yes, you'll have to get a bit messy eating it, but that's part of the experience. Chicken drumsticks are one of the cheapest cuts of chicken but they also have the most flavour. This is a recipe I watched being made in Kerala and I liked it so much, it was one of the first curries I made when I got home.

PREP TIME: 15 MINS
COOKING TIME: 30 MINS

15 chicken drumsticks, skinned, with shallow slits cut into the meat
1 tsp ground turmeric

FOR THE SPICE MASALA
1 tbsp cumin seeds
1 tbsp coriander seeds
2 tsp fennel seeds
2.5cm (1in) cinnamon stick
1 tbsp black peppercorns

FOR THE CURRY
7 garlic cloves, smashed
5cm (2in) piece of ginger, roughly chopped
2–3 green finger chillies, roughly chopped
2 large onions, roughly chopped
200g (7oz) chopped tomatoes
4 tbsp rapeseed (canola) oil
2 tsp mustard seeds
20 fresh or frozen curry leaves, plus extra (optional) to garnish
1 tbsp Kashmiri chilli powder (more or less to taste)
1 small bunch of coriander (cilantro), finely chopped
400ml (1½ cups) tinned (canned) thick coconut milk
Salt, to taste
2 limes, quartered, to serve

Mix the chicken legs with the turmeric so that the legs are evenly coated. Set aside.

Place the cumin, coriander and fennel seeds, cinnamon stick and peppercorns in a frying pan (skillet) and toast over a medium–high heat until warm to the touch and fragrant. Be careful not to burn them. Using a spice grinder or pestle and mortar, grind all of these spices into a fine powder. Set aside.

Place the garlic, ginger and green chillies in a small food processor and blend with a little water into a paste. Set aside.

Now blend the onions and tomatoes together to form another smooth paste and again set aside. Heat the oil in a large pan or wok over a medium–high heat. When small bubbles start forming at the bottom of the pan and rise to the top, add the mustard seeds. When the seeds begin to crackle, toss in the curry leaves.

Let these sizzle for about 30 seconds and then stir in the garlic, ginger and chilli paste. Stir in the prepared spice masala and the Kashmiri chilli powder and continue cooking for another minute.

Fry, stirring continuously, for about 30 seconds and then pour in the onion/tomato paste. Fry this, stirring often, for about 5 minutes or until this base masala has turned a couple of tones darker.

Add the chicken legs and stir them in so that they are coated with the base masala ingredients. Now add the chopped coriander (cilantro), followed by the coconut milk. Bring to a simmer and cover the pan. Reduce the heat to medium and simmer for 10 minutes.

Lift the lid and continue simmering to thicken the sauce until you are happy with the consistency and the chicken is cooked through.

Check for seasoning and add salt to taste. Garnish with a handful of fresh curry leaves, if you like, and serve with the quartered limes over rice.

BANGALORE GREEN CHILLI CHICKEN CURRY

SERVES 4

This is a curry I tried during a very short and unplanned trip to Bangalore. I was told that the recipe was inspired by a popular green chilli curry from Andhra but with a few special amendments by the chef. He used more green chillies, which made the curry really spicy, and a little coconut milk to cool it down while still retaining the fresh flavour of all those green chillies. The curry was served with chicken that was cut into small pieces on the bone, but here I have used boneless for easier eating.

PREP TIME: 15 MINS
COOKING TIME: 30 MINS

2 tbsp rapeseed (canola) oil
5cm (2in) cinnamon stick
10 black peppercorns
3 green cardamom pods, lightly crushed
2 black cardamom pods, lightly crushed
2 medium red onions, very finely chopped
10 green finger chillies, finely chopped (to taste)
½ tsp ground turmeric
2 tsp ground coriander
1 tsp ground cumin
2 medium tomatoes, finely diced
1 g (2lb 2oz) skinless chicken thighs, cut into bite-sized pieces
125ml (½ cup) thick coconut milk
125ml (¼ cup) water or chicken stock (optional)
½ tsp garam masala (see page 161)
Salt and pepper, to taste
4 tbsp coriander (cilantro), finely chopped, to garnish

FOR THE CHILLI PASTE

3 tbsp rapeseed (canola) oil
12 green bird's eye chillies
2 garlic cloves, peeled
1 medium red onion, roughly chopped
1 large bunch of coriander (cilantro), roughly chopped
1 small bunch of mint leaves, roughly chopped
Juice of 1 lime
About 70ml (¼ cup) water

To make the chilli paste, heat the oil over a medium–high heat in a frying pan (skillet) or saucepan that has a lid and add the chillies, garlic and the roughly chopped onion. Fry for about 5 minutes or until the onion and garlic are turning soft and the chillies are blistering in places. Using a slotted spoon, transfer these ingredients to a food processor or large spice grinder and add the coriander (cilantro) and mint leaves. Squeeze in the lime juice and add enough of the water to blend to a very smooth, green paste.

You should still have a little oil in your pan. Add more as needed, until you have about 70ml (¼ cup) oil in the pan, and then add the whole spices. Fry to infuse these flavours into the oil for about a minute and then tip in the finely chopped onions. Stir well to coat with the oil and fry for about 7 minutes or until the onions are soft, translucent and just beginning to brown.

Stir in the chopped chillies. Careful here, you don't want to add them all if you don't like a really spicy curry! Continue to fry for a few more minutes to darken the onions until they are golden brown in colour. Stir in the ground turmeric, coriander and cumin and stir well to combine. Then add the chopped tomatoes and stir them in. Add the chicken thighs and stir some more until the meat is turning white on the exterior.

Cover the pan and cook over a medium heat for about 10 minutes, lifting the lid a couple of times to stir. Now add the green chilli paste and stir it in. Cover again and simmer over a medium heat for another 5 minutes. Lift the lid, add the coconut milk and stir it in. The curry will be quite thick but you can add a little water or chicken stock if you prefer more sauce. Cover the pan again for 5 minutes. Add the garam masala and season to taste with salt and pepper. Serve hot, garnished with coriander (cilantro).

CHICKEN SHAHI KORMA

SERVES 4–6

This korma is actually just a variation of the popular shahi kofta korma on page 68, where the red-coloured gravy is replaced with a delicate white version. The curry can be traced back to the Mughal era of the Indian subcontinent. Shahi, which means royal in Hindi, indicates that this dish and other shahi recipes were associated with the royal kitchens of the Mughal emperors.

PREP TIME: 15 MINS
COOKING TIME: 45 MINS

1kg (2lb 2oz) chicken (I used legs and thighs on the bone), skinned and cut into small pieces
1 tbsp Kashmiri chilli powder
120ml (½ cup) natural yoghurt
70ml (¼ cup) rapeseed (canola) oil
2 tbsp ghee
2 medium red onions, thinly sliced and cut into 2.5cm (1in) pieces
40g (½ cup) flaked (slivered) almonds, soaked in water for about 10 minutes or longer
2 tbsp garlic and ginger paste
1–3 green finger chillies, finely chopped (optional for more heat)
½ tsp cumin seeds
2.5cm (1in) cinnamon stick
1 Indian bay leaf (cassia leaf)
10 black peppercorns
3 green cardamom pods, smashed and seeds removed
2 cloves
About 70ml (¼ cup) water
1½ tbsp garam masala (see page 161) or good-quality shop-bought
Salt, to taste
Chopped coriander (cilantro) and/or toasted flaked (slivered) almonds, to garnish

Put the chicken pieces in a mixing bowl and add the chilli powder, ½ teaspoon of salt and 2 tablespoons of the yoghurt and mix well with your hands until the chicken is evenly coated in the marinade. Allow to marinate while you prepare the rest of the dish.

Heat the rapeseed (canola) oil and ghee in a karahi or large saucepan over a medium–high heat. When the oil appears to quiver slightly, stir in the sliced onions and sprinkle ½ teaspoon of salt over them, which will help caramelize them. Fry, stirring regularly, for 10–15 minutes or until the onions are a deep golden brown. Transfer the fried onions to a plate to cool. Set aside.

At this point, you could discard all but about 3 tablespoons of the oil and ghee in the pan but it would be left in when cooked the traditional way. Add the marinated chicken to the hot fat and fry over a medium–high heat for about 10 minutes or until nicely browned and about 80 per cent cooked through.

While you are cooking the chicken, prepare the korma paste. (This and frying the onions can be done up to a day before cooking if more convenient.) Place the soaked flaked (slivered) almonds, garlic and ginger paste, fried onions, green chillies, if using, and the remaining yoghurt in a food processor and blend to a smooth, creamy paste. If needed you can add a drop of water to do this. Set aside.

Returning to the chicken, it should be nicely browned and almost cooked through, sizzling in that flavoured oil. Stir in the whole spices and fry for about a minute to infuse their flavour into the oil. Then stir in the korma paste. Be sure to get it all by adding the water to your blender and swishing it around to get the paste from the sides, then pour that in too.

Stir it all up so that the chicken is coated with the korma sauce, then cover the pan and simmer over a low–medium heat for 15 minutes. When you lift the lid, the oil will have separated from the sauce and will be floating on top. That is how this korma should look but feel free to skim off some of that oil if you want.

Try the curry and season with salt to taste. Stir in the garam masala and serve garnished with chopped coriander (cilantro) and/or toasted flaked almonds.

WHITE CHICKEN SHAHI KOFTA KORMA

SERVES 4–6

White chicken shahi korma is a rich and creamy curry which is actually just a variation of the popular chicken shahi korma on page 66 but the traditional red-coloured gravy is replaced with a delicate white gravy. If you like this curry, you are going to want to try the hotel (restaurant) style white gravy on page 158 too.

PREP TIME: 20 MINS
COOKING TIME: 20 MINS

700g (1lb 9oz) minced (ground)
   chicken
1 tbsp garlic and ginger paste
1 red onion, very finely chopped
1 tsp ground cumin
1 tsp ground coriander
1 tsp red pepper flakes
2 green finger chillies,
   finely chopped
½ tsp garam masala
   (see page 161)
1 tsp ground black pepper
2 slices of white bread,
   crusts removed
2 tbsp natural yoghurt
2 tbsp single (light) cream
½ tsp salt
2 tbsp coriander (cilantro),
   finely chopped
70ml (¼ cup) rapeseed (canola)
   oil or ghee

FOR THE CURRY

2 medium red onions, chopped
2 tbsp garlic and ginger paste
15 cashews
1½ tbsp melon seeds (optional)
6 whole green finger chillies
   (more or less to taste)
120ml (½ cup) natural yoghurt
3 cardamom pods, bruised
½ tsp ground black pepper
½ tsp garam masala
1 tsp ground cumin
1 tsp kasoori methi (dried
   fenugreek leaves)
70ml (¼ cup) single (light)
   cream, plus more to garnish
3 tbsp coriander (cilantro),
   finely chopped, to garnish

Mix the chicken with all the kofta ingredients up to and including the coriander (cilantro). It is important to really break the chicken down with your hands so that it is silky smooth, so spend some time kneading it for a couple of minutes. With wet hands, divide the chicken into balls (kofta) that are just a bit smaller than pool balls. Rolling the balls with wet hands will not only make the job easier but you will get a nice smooth surface.

Heat the oil in a frying pan (skillet) over a medium–high heat. When tiny bubbles form and sizzling sounds can be heard from the oil, add the kofta and fry for a few minutes until they are about 80 per cent cooked through and browned in places. Traditionally, the same oil is used to cook the curry but you could pour some out if you don't want an oil-heavy curry.

With the oil still hot, continue cooking over a medium–high heat and add the chopped onions. Fry for about 5 minutes or until soft and translucent, then add the garlic and ginger paste, cashews, melon seeds, if using, and chillies. Fry for another couple of minutes. You want to cook the nuts and seeds a bit but not necessarily brown them, so just an easy couple of minutes is all that's needed. Take off the heat and transfer this all to a bowl with a slotted spoon and allow to cool a little. Then place it all in a blender and blend with the yoghurt into a smooth, creamy white paste.

Returning to your pan, heat the oil again over a medium–high heat and add the cardamom pods to sizzle and flavour the oil for about 30 seconds. Then pour in the prepared white paste and stir well to combine with the oil. Add the black pepper, garam masala, ground cumin, kasoori methi (dried fenugreek leaves) and cream and stir to combine. Return the par-cooked koftas and bring it all to a simmer. Cover the pan and simmer over a medium heat for about 5 minutes. The oil will separate from the gravy and float on top. Try the sauce and add salt to taste. Spoon it all into a heated serving dish, drizzle with a little more cream and garnish with the chopped coriander.

CHICKEN CHANGEZI
SERVES 4–6

I tried this curry while on a food tour of Old Delhi with my friend Anubhav Sapra from Delhi Food Walks. At a restaurant called Al Maaidah – Changezi Chicken, which is believed to be the first restaurant to introduce the now famous curry, I finally got to enjoy this curry the way it's meant to be. At Al Maaidah, long spits of marinated chickens are roasted on rotisseries and then pieces of the meat are torn off and added to the delicious changezi sauce. Below I have simplified this but feel free to use spit-roast tandoori chicken instead, if you're feeling ambitious.

PREP TIME: 10 MINS
COOKING TIME: 50 MINS

FOR THE CHICKEN
1kg (2lb 2oz) chicken, on the
  bone, cut into small pieces
½–1 tsp salt
Juice of 1 lemon
1½ tbsp Kashmiri chilli powder
2 tsp ground cumin
2 tsp ground coriander
3 tbsp garlic, ginger and chilli
  paste (see page 161)
3 tbsp ghee

FOR THE CURRY
2 tbsp ghee
3 red onions, very finely chopped
½ tsp salt
4 tbsp garlic, ginger and chilli
  paste (see page 161)
½ tsp ground turmeric
1 tbsp Kashmiri chilli powder
1 tsp chaat masala (optional)
1 tbsp ground cumin
1 tbsp ground coriander
1 tsp amchoor powder
70ml (¼ cup) water or stock
600ml (2½ cups) passata
70ml (¼ cup) mustard oil
  (optional)
4 tbsp natural yoghurt, whisked
4 tbsp single (light) cream
1 tsp garam masala (see page 161)
1 tsp kasoori methi (dried
  fenugreek leaves)
Salt, to taste

TO GARNISH (OPTIONAL)
4 green bird's eye chillies, sliced
  lengthwise into fine strips
1 lemon, quartered
2.5cm (1in) piece of ginger,
  peeled and julienned

Place the chicken pieces in a mixing bowl and add all the marinade ingredients up to and including the garlic, ginger and chilli paste. Rub the marinade right into the flesh and set aside to marinate for 20 minutes, or just go straight to cooking.

Heat the ghee in a large frying pan (skillet) that has a lid over a medium–high heat. When the oil is sizzling hot, add the chicken and fry for about 4 minutes, then turn the pieces to brown the other side. Reduce the heat to low, cover the pan and cook for a further 10 minutes or until the chicken is about 80 per cent cooked through. Cooking the chicken this way will make it caramelize on the bottom of the pan. Transfer to a bowl and pour all the juices from the pan over the chicken. Set aside.

Now let's make the curry! Heat the ghee in a large frying pan over a medium–high heat. When visibly hot, stir in the chopped onions and salt and fry, stirring regularly, for about 8 minutes or until they are golden brown in colour. Add the garlic, ginger and chilli paste and fry for a further minute. Stir in the ground spices and then pour in the water or stock so that the spices don't burn and bring to a simmer.

Add the passata and bring to a simmer. Cover the pan and continue simmering over a medium heat for about 20 minutes. Your changezi gravy is ready, so you could just stir in the yoghurt and cream, then add the chicken and salt to taste at this point and enjoy. If you want to make it street food-style, however, you have a few more steps.

In another large frying pan, heat the mustard oil over a medium–high heat. When visibly sizzling hot, add the prepared gravy one ladle at a time and let it all come to a simmer. Stir in the yoghurt, one tablespoon at a time, then stir in the cream. Sprinkle in the garam masala and kasoori methi (dried fenugreek leaves) and season with salt to taste. Stir in the cooked chicken and bring the sauce to a bubbling simmer to heat the chicken through, ensuring the chicken is nicely coated with the sauce and then add all or some garnishes of your choice.

KARI AYAM JAWA
SERVES 4

The first influence of Indian cuisine on Indonesian cooking can be traced back as far as the 4th century. So long before chillies made their way to the Far East. Kari ayam jawa, or Javanese chicken curry, has been made in this way for centuries. Although chillies and/or chilli powder are sometimes added to the curry paste nowadays, it is much more common to be served a Kari ayam jawa the way it was originally made, without chillies. Personally, I like to prepare the curry just like this but usually either garnish it with fresh chopped chillies or serve them on the side. Chicken powder is often added to Southeast Asian dishes. It contains MSG, so is optional, but it also adds a delicious flavour. This is served as a soup but if you want a few carbs, try serving it with chapattis or boiled potatoes.

PREP TIME: 15 MINS
COOKING TIME: 20 MINS

1 x 1.5kg (3lb 5oz) chicken, cut into 8 pieces
1 lemon, quartered
1 tsp salt
1 tsp Asian chicken powder (contains MSG, optional)

FOR THE CURRY PASTE
6 shallots, roughly chopped
1 lemongrass stalk, woody exterior removed, white part only, thinly sliced
6 garlic cloves, smashed
2.5cm (1in) piece of ginger, roughly chopped
3 candlenuts or macadamia nuts
1 generous tsp ground coriander
1 generous tsp ground cumin
½ tsp ground turmeric

FOR THE CURRY
2 tbsp rapeseed (canola) oil
2.5cm (1in) cinnamon stick
1 lemongrass stalk, woody exterior removed, white part only, lightly smashed
3 makrut lime leaves
250ml (1 cup) water or chicken stock
400ml (1½ cups) coconut milk
Sugar, to taste
Salt, to taste

TO GARNISH
2 red spur chillies, thinly sliced (optional)
3 tbsp coriander (cilantro), finely chopped (optional)

Place the chicken pieces in a mixing bowl and squeeze the lemon juice all over them. Add the salt and chicken powder, if using, and mix well with your hands so that the chicken is nicely coated. Set aside.

Place the curry paste ingredients in a blender and add just enough water to blend into a smooth, thick paste. Set aside.

Now heat a frying pan (skillet) or wok over a medium–high heat and add the oil. Once you feel the heat radiating from the hot oil in the pan when you hold your hand over it, add the cinnamon stick, lemongrass and lime leaves and let their flavours infuse into the oil for about 30 seconds. Then pour in the prepared curry paste and fry, stirring regularly, for about 3 minutes to cook out the rawness. Add the chicken pieces and stir well until the chicken is thoroughly coated with the curry paste.

Stir in the water or chicken stock and bring to a simmer. Cover the pan and continue simmering for 15 minutes or until the chicken is cooked through. Uncover and add the coconut milk, then bring back to a simmer to thicken. Continue simmering until you are happy with the sauce consistency. Try it and add sugar and salt to taste. To add a bit of colour, you can garnish with thinly sliced spur chillies and/or chopped coriander (cilantro).

KOREAN SPICY RAMEN
SERVES 4

I'm a huge fan of ramen, and this spicy chicken ramen is one I make when I want a lot of flavour but have no desire to cook. I cook most days, for my blog and also to test recipes for books, so when I do take a day off, I want something that can be thrown together quickly without really needing to think about it. This spicy ramen is one such easy meal. Ramen is, of course, Japanese in origin but the Koreans have taken many ramen dishes and really made them their own. I usually use instant ramen noodles for this recipe but you could use better-quality ramen. Just follow the cooking instructions on the packaging.

PREP TIME: 10 MINS
COOKING TIME: 15 MINS

FOR THE RAMEN
4 eggs (optional)
700g (1lb 9oz) chicken thighs, skin removed and cut into small bite-sized pieces
1 tbsp sesame oil
1 medium onion, finely chopped
6 chestnut mushrooms, thinly sliced, or 1 handful of enoki mushrooms
2 litres (4 cups) unsalted chicken stock
450g (1lb) dried ramen noodles
Salt, to taste

FOR THE MARINADE
2 tsp sesame oil
3½ tbsp gochujang (Korean hot pepper paste, more or less to taste)
1 tbsp gochugaru (Korean hot pepper flakes, more or less to taste)
2 tbsp white miso
2 tbsp garlic and ginger paste
2 tbsp light soy sauce or tamari

TO GARNISH
3 spring onions (scallions), thinly sliced into rings
Extra vegetables of choice (optional)
4 red bird's eye chillies, slit down the middle (optional)
4 tbsp coriander (cilantro), finely chopped (optional)

If adding the optional eggs, boil them for 6–8 minutes or to your preferred doneness. Six minutes will get you a soft yolk and 8 minutes will have a harder yolk, but cooking times can vary depending on the size of your eggs. Place the cooked eggs in ice-cold water to stop them cooking further. Then peel them and slice in half lengthwise. If they turn cold, they will heat up again in the ramen broth.

In a mixing bowl, whisk all the marinade ingredients together and stir in the chicken. Allow to marinate while you fry the onion or for up to 4 hours if convenient. Now heat the tablespoon of sesame oil in a large saucepan over a medium heat. Stir in the finely chopped onion and chestnut mushrooms and fry for about 5 minutes to soften. If you are using enoki mushrooms, these should be added just before serving as they cook through really quickly. Add the marinated chicken with all the marinade and fry for about 3 minutes, stirring regularly until it is about 80 per cent cooked through.

Pour in the stock and bring to a simmer over a medium–high heat. While the stock is coming to a simmer, begin soaking your ramen noodles as per the packet instructions. Be sure not to let them soak too long or they will fall apart and become mushy. You want them to be a bit al dente as they will continue to cook in the hot broth. Taste some of the broth and adjust the flavouring. Season with salt to taste.

Divide the noodles between four large ramen bowls. Top with some of the chicken and broth and add the eggs, if using. Garnish with the chopped spring onions (scallions) and more veggies, such as red (bell) pepper, as well as fresh chillies or coriander (cilantro) if you like.

SZECHUAN CHICKEN
SERVES 4

When I go out for Chinese food, I always order Szechuan chicken. I find the numbing sensation in the Szechuan peppercorns addictive and love pretty much any Chinese dish that includes them. Often the chicken pieces are cut much smaller than I do in this recipe, but I prefer them this way. You could always adjust to preference. Szechuan chicken is usually quite spicy and this version is even more so with the use of garlic chilli oil and paste. The dried chillies aren't meant to be eaten but are quite spicy and nice if you want to give them a try.

PREP TIME: 10 MINS
COOKING TIME: 20 MINS

700g (1lb 9oz) boneless chicken thighs, skinned and cut into 2.5cm (1in) pieces
2 tbsp Chinese rice wine
2 tbsp light soy sauce or tamari
3 tbsp rice flour
30g (¼ cup) cornflour (cornstarch)

FOR THE SAUCE
3 tbsp light soy sauce or tamari
1 tbsp hoisin sauce
1 tbsp sesame oil
1 tbsp brown sugar
1 tbsp cornflour (cornstarch)
100ml (⅓ cup) chicken stock

FOR THE STIR-FRY
Rapeseed (canola) oil, for shallow-frying
1 tbsp finely chopped garlic
1 tbsp finely chopped ginger
1 tbsp spring onions (scallions), thinly sliced
1 onion, quartered and cut into 2.5cm (1in) petals
1 red (bell) pepper, seeded and cut into 2.5cm (1in) pieces
1 green (bell) pepper, seeded and cut into 2.5cm (1in) pieces
1 tbsp Szechuan peppercorns, lightly crushed
15 small dried red Chinese or bird's eye chillies
1 tsp white pepper
2 tbsp toasted sesame seeds

Start by preparing the sauce. Whisk all the sauce ingredients in a mixing bowl until smooth. Set aside.

Now place the chicken pieces in a mixing bowl and add the rice wine and soy sauce or tamari. You can cook almost immediately or allow to marinate overnight in the fridge for even better results.

Place the rice flour and cornflour (cornstarch) on a plate and then dust the marinated chicken pieces with the flour. Be sure to shake off any excess flour.

Heat about 2.5cm (1in) of rapeseed (canola) oil in a wok and place over a medium–high heat. The oil needs to reach 180°C (350°F) before adding the chicken. If you don't have an oil thermometer, place the end of a wooden chopstick or spatula in the oil. If bubbles begin to sizzle around the wood immediately, your oil is ready.

Cook the flour-coated chicken in small batches. If you add too many pieces, it will cool the oil, so don't do that. Fry each batch until the chicken is lightly browned and crispy. Transfer to a rack to drain off any excess oil. Each batch should take about 5 minutes.

Pour out the oil and clean your wok with paper towels. Then add about 1 tablespoon of oil and fry the garlic, ginger and spring onions (scallions) for about 30 seconds.

Add the onion, (bell) peppers and Szechuan peppercorns and fry for about a minute or until the veggies are just cooked through and still a bit crisp. Stir in the dried chillies, white pepper and sauce and bring to a simmer. Then return the fried chicken to the wok and stir to coat in the sauce. Sprinkle with sesame seeds and serve.

GOAN-STYLE CHICKEN VINDALOO
SERVES 4

Most people who love curry know that Vindaloo originated in Goa and is made with pork. That is the original version but the Goans also love the vindaloo sauce with other meats such as chicken, duck, buffalo and beef. This chicken vindaloo can be prepared much faster and is equally as delicious as any pork vindaloo out there.

PREP TIME: 30 MINS,
PLUS MARINATING
COOKING TIME: 30 MINS

1kg (2lb 2oz) chicken thighs on the bone, skinned and chopped in half
2–3 tbsp coconut or rapeseed (canola) oil
1 head of garlic, cloves cut into slivers
1 teaspoon brown or black mustard seeds
20 fresh curry leaves
2 onions, finely chopped
3 tomatoes, finely chopped (about 400g/14oz)
1 tsp chilli powder (more or less to taste)
2 Indian bay leaves (cassia leaves)
Juice of 1 lime, or to taste
Salt, to taste

FOR THE VINDALOO
MARINADE
3 dried red chillies
1 tbsp cumin seeds
1 tbsp coriander seeds
1 tsp black cardamom seeds
1 tsp fenugreek seeds
5 cloves
2.5cm (1in) piece of cassia bark
10 black peppercorns
½ tsp ground turmeric
4 green chillies, finely chopped
75ml (¼ cup) red wine vinegar (plus more if needed)
1 tbsp tamarind paste (or another 2 tbsp vinegar)
2 tbsp soft brown sugar
2 tbsp garlic and ginger paste

Start by preparing the marinade. Place all the dry spices, except the turmeric, in a dry frying pan (skillet) over a medium heat and toast until they become fragrant and warm to the touch but are not yet smoking. Transfer to a plate to cool slightly, then pour them into a spice grinder or food processor with the turmeric and grind to a fine powder. You could also use a pestle and mortar but that's a lot more work.

Add the chillies, vinegar, tamarind paste, brown sugar and garlic and ginger paste and blend to a smooth vindaloo marinade paste. Put the chicken in a large bowl with the marinade and stir well to combine. Leave to marinate for 30 minutes or up to 4 hours.

When ready to cook, heat the oil in a saucepan, large frying pan or wok over a low heat. Add the garlic slivers and allow to cook gently for about 10 minutes or until crispy and light golden brown in colour. It is important not to burn the garlic, so watch it carefully. Using a slotted spoon, transfer the garlic to a plate and set aside.

Using the same oil, heat your pan over a medium–high heat until the oil is beginning to shimmer. Add the mustard seeds and when they begin to crackle, stir in the curry leaves. Fry for about 30 seconds until the leaves are very fragrant and then toss in the chopped onions.

Fry for about 5 minutes over a medium–high heat until the onions are soft and translucent. Sprinkle a little salt over the onions. This will help release moisture from them. Add the chopped tomatoes, chilli powder, bay leaves and the chicken with its marinade and then pour in just enough water to cover.

Leave to simmer for about 10 minutes. Give it all a good stir, then cover the pan and continue simmering over a medium heat for a further 8 minutes. Uncover the pan and continue simmering to reduce the sauce and thicken it a little.

To serve, stir in the fried garlic. Try the curry and add salt to taste. You can also adjust other spicing at this time such as additional chilli powder. Just be sure to simmer it in the sauce for a couple of minutes to cook out the raw flavour. Add lime juice to taste and serve over white rice.

PUNJABI GINGER CHICKEN CURRY

SERVES 4

One thing I like to do when developing recipes like this hugely popular Punjabi-style curry is to make them as authentic as possible. You might notice in the instructions below that I use quite a lot of oil. This is about half as much oil as this curry is usually made with. The oil gives the curry a delicious shine when served but, of course, it's not a good idea for the health conscious, so feel free to reduce the amount of oil if you like. Either way, if you love ginger, you've got to give this ginger chicken curry, or Murgh andraki, a try!

PREP TIME: 10 MINS
COOKING TIME: 20 MINS

80ml (⅓ cup) rapeseed
  (canola) oil
2.5cm (1in) cinnamon stick
1 Indian bay leaf (cassia
  leaf, optional)
2 medium red onions,
  finely chopped
2 tbsp garlic and ginger paste
2 green bird's eye chillies,
  finely chopped
2.5cm (1in) piece of ginger,
  roughly chopped
700g (1lb 9oz) skinned chicken
  thighs, cut small on the bone
1 tsp salt
2 tsp Kashmiri chilli powder
1 tsp dried red chilli flakes
½ tsp ground turmeric
1 tsp coriander seeds,
  lightly crushed
1 tsp ground coriander
1 tsp ground cumin
200g (7oz) tinned (canned)
  chopped tomatoes
100ml (6½ tbsp) natural yoghurt
7.5cm (3in) piece of ginger,
  peeled and julienned
About 125ml (½ cup) water
1 tsp kasoori methi (dried
  fenugreek leaves)
Salt and pepper, to taste
3 tbsp fresh coriander (cilantro),
  finely chopped, to serve

Heat the oil over a medium–high heat in a pan that has a lid. When it is starting to bubble, stir in the cinnamon stick and the Indian bay leaf, if using. Allow these spices to infuse into the oil for about 30 seconds and then add the chopped onions. Fry the onions for about 7 minutes or until soft, translucent and just beginning to turn a golden brown. Stir in the garlic and ginger paste, chillies and the roughly chopped ginger and fry for a further 30 seconds.

Now add the chicken to the pan and stir well to coat with the onion mixture. Add the salt, chilli powder, chilli flakes, turmeric, coriander seeds, ground coriander and cumin and stir well to combine.

Pour in the chopped tomatoes and then add the yoghurt, one tablespoon at a time, stirring as you do. Add about half the julienned ginger and pour in just enough water to cover. Cover the pan and simmer for 15 minutes or until the chicken is cooked through and you have thickish sauce.

Take off the lid and continue simmering until you are happy with the consistency of the sauce, which should be rather thick and clinging to the chicken pieces, but you can add more water or chicken stock if you prefer more sauce. Add the kasoori methi (dried fenugreek leaves) by rubbing them between your fingers and into the sauce. Season with salt and pepper to taste. The flavours of black pepper and ginger go well together, so I tend to add quite a lot of pepper but please do this to taste. Garnish with the chopped coriander (cilantro) and remaining julienned ginger to serve.

VIETNAMESE WHOLE BOILED CHICKEN

SERVES 4

Chicken boiled in this way is Chinese in origin where it's called Hainanese chicken. It is, however, popular all over Southeast Asia, with each country giving it their own touch. When Caroline and I tried this at a restaurant in Hanoi, Vietnam, it was a real showpiece. The whole chicken, including the head, feet and innards, was served on a platter with rice and a few dipping sauces. In many Western countries, finding whole chickens like this is a thing of the past, so you can use a headless and footless chicken as well as leaving out the innards.

PREP TIME: 15 MINS
COOKING TIME: 1 HOUR

1 x 1.5–2kg (3lb 5oz–4½lb)
   free-range whole chicken
1 tbsp salt
2 lemongrass stalks,
   lightly smashed
3 spring onions (scallions)
8 garlic cloves, lightly smashed
5cm (2in) piece of ginger,
   lightly smashed
1 tsp ground turmeric

Carefully open the cavity of the chicken and remove as much of the fat from inside as you can and set aside for later. Rub the salt all over the exterior and inside the cavity of the chicken. Stuff the cavity with the lemongrass, spring onions (scallions), garlic and ginger and tie the legs together to keep these aromatic ingredients inside the bird. This can be done a day or so ahead of cooking if more convenient.

When ready to cook, fill a pot that has a tight-fitting lid three-quarters full with water. Be sure to use a pot that is large enough to submerge the chicken completely in the water. Place the chicken in the water and cover with the lid. Bring to the boil over a high heat. Once boiling, watch it carefully as you only want to boil the chicken for 15 minutes.

After 15 minutes of boiling, turn off the heat and let it continue cooking for another 30–45 minutes in the hot water. You can check for doneness by sticking a toothpick into the thigh. If the juices run clear, which they should after that amount of time in the water, your chicken is cooked.

While the chicken is cooking, you can prepare the glaze. Melt the chicken fat you removed earlier in a pan over a medium–high heat. This will take about 15–20 minutes. Once you have a good amount of rendered fat, stir in the ground turmeric and stir until it has a nice golden glow and set aside.

Once your chicken is cooked through, brush the turmeric-coloured chicken fat all over the exterior of the chicken. Serve with white rice and a couple of dipping sauces such as equal amounts of flaky salt and freshly ground pepper made into a dipping condiment with lime juice squeezed over the top and nu'ó'c châ'm (see page 163). The light stock produced while cooking the chicken can be served on the side too, or refrigerated/frozen for later use in another recipe.

CHICKEN ROGAN JOSH (CHICKEN ROGHANI)

SERVES 4

Rogan josh is traditionally prepared with mutton or goat meat and originates from the Kashmir region of India and Pakistan. At curry houses, any protein can be added to the rogan josh sauce and it is still called rogan josh. This is a recipe for chicken roghani, which is the name given in India and Pakistan when chicken is used. The spicing is the same, though some ingredients can vary depending on who is making it. Kashmiri Muslims use a lot of onions and garlic. Non-Muslims in the Kashmir don't cook with onions and garlic and add other spices to compensate. It's the Muslim version that is closest to what is served at curry houses, so that is what you're going to get in this recipe.

PREP TIME: 20 MINS
COOKING TIME: 20 MINS

85ml (6 tbsp) ghee or
    mustard oil
2 Indian bay leaves
    (cassia leaves)
1 tsp cumin seeds
2 medium onions, very
    finely chopped
2 tbsp garlic and ginger paste
70ml (¼ cup) unseasoned
    passata
70ml (¼ cup) water
1kg (2lb 2oz) chicken thighs and
    chicken legs, skinned
1 tsp garam masala
    (see page 161)
Salt, to taste
4 tbsp coriander (cilantro),
    finely chopped, to garnish

FOR THE ROGHANI MASALA

1 tbsp fennel seeds
2.5cm (1in) cinnamon stick
3 black cardamom pods
4 green cardamom pods
4 cloves
3 tbsp Kashmiri chilli powder,
    paprika or a blend of the two
1 tbsp ground coriander
½ tsp ground ginger

Grind the whole spices for the roghani masala to a fine powder in a spice grinder or pestle and mortar. Stir in the chilli powder, ground coriander and ginger and set aside.

When ready to cook, heat the ghee or mustard oil in a large pan over a medium–high heat. Stir in the bay leaves and cumin seeds and allow them to flavour the hot oil for about 30 seconds. Then stir in the chopped onions and fry for about 8 minutes or until they are golden brown in colour. Stir in the garlic and ginger paste and fry it for 30 seconds, then add the roghani masala spice blend and fry and stir it into the onions. Add the passata and water, bring it all to a simmer and then add the chicken.

Give it all a good stir to coat the chicken with the sauce, then cover the pan, reduce the heat to low–medium and simmer for 20 minutes, giving it a good stir halfway through.

After 20 minutes, lift the lid. All that oil or ghee will be a shiny red floating on top. Stir in the garam masala and season with salt to taste. Scoop deep into the curry to plate it up and drizzle some of the red ghee or oil over the top of each serving. Garnish with chopped coriander (cilantro) and serve with rice, naans or chapattis.

KOREAN CHICKEN STEW
SERVES 4

This hearty chicken stew, or Dakdoritang, makes a delicious weekday meal. It's really easy to prepare and will be on your table in less than an hour. I personally don't find Korean gochujang (red spice paste) or gochugaru (Korean chilli flakes) very spicy, so I add quite a lot. If you're not sure about the spiciness, add less. You can always stir more in to taste before serving.

PREP TIME: 15 MINS
COOKING TIME: 30 MINS

8 new potatoes, sliced in half
1.5kg (3lb 5oz) skinless chicken
   thighs on the bone, cut in half
1 large carrot, cut into 2.5cm
   (1in) chunks
1 onion, quartered and then
   divided into individual petals
10 garlic cloves, lightly crushed
2.5cm (1in) piece of ginger,
   peeled and julienned
3 spring onions (scallions),
   roughly chopped
1–2 spur chillies, thinly sliced
   to preference
2 tbsp sesame oil
1 tbsp sesame seeds

FOR THE BROTH
500ml (2 cups) chicken stock
   or water
5 tbsp light soy sauce
2 tbsp gochujang (Korean hot
   pepper paste), or to taste
3 tbsp gochugaru (Korean hot
   pepper flakes), or to taste
3 tbsp Chinese rice wine or
   dry sherry
½ tsp ground black pepper
1 tbsp sugar

Pour the stock or water into a large saucepan and stir in all of the remaining broth ingredients.

Bring this to a rolling simmer over a high heat and then add the potatoes and chicken. Bring back to a simmer, then reduce the heat to medium and cover the pan. Simmer for 15 minutes to cook the chicken through.

Add the carrot, onion, garlic and ginger and continue to simmer, covered, for another 10 minutes, stirring from time to time. Now remove the lid and continue simmering for another 5–10 minutes to thicken the sauce and cook the vegetables through.

Just before serving, stir in the spring onions (scallions) and spur chillies, along with the sesame oil. Garnish with the sesame seeds to serve.

SRI LANKAN CHICKEN CURRY
SERVES 4

This is one of the first Sri Lankan recipes I ever made. I learned the recipe back in 2016 while in Colombo. In fact, I learned it a few times as it was very popular at different restaurants and each chef put their own spin on it. I actually featured a similar recipe in my book *The Curry Guy Light* but this is not a light version. Although this recipe is closer to what is served all over Sri Lanka, it is still quite healthy and, of course, amazing.

PREP TIME: 15 MINS
COOKING TIME: 30 MINS

3 tbsp coconut oil
1 tsp black mustard seeds
1 cinnamon stick
1 tsp cumin seeds
3 cloves
5 green cardamom pods, lightly bruised
2 bay leaves
7.5cm (3in) pandan leaf, cut into 3 strips
20 curry leaves
2 onions, finely chopped
2 tbsp garlic and ginger paste
3 green chillies (whichever you prefer)
1 tsp ground turmeric
1 tsp ground cumin
1 tsp ground coriander
1 tsp red chilli powder
1–2 tbsp finely ground black pepper (to taste)
1kg (2lb 2oz) chicken thighs, cut into bite-sized pieces
2 sweet green peppers (banana chillies are used in Sri Lanka)
2 medium tomatoes, diced
1 red onion, thinly sliced
70ml (¼ cup) water or chicken stock
2 tbsp light soy sauce or tamari (optional)
400ml (1½ cups) thick coconut milk
Salt, to taste

Heat the coconut oil in a large wok or pan until bubbling hot. Stir in the mustard seeds and, when they begin to crackle, stir in the cinnamon stick, cumin seeds, cloves, cardamom pods, bay leaves, pandan leaf and curry leaves. Let these flavours infuse into the hot oil for about 40 seconds and then add the chopped onions.

Fry the chopped onions for about 5 minutes or until soft and translucent and then stir in the garlic and ginger paste, green chillies and the ground spices. I recommend adding only about 1 teaspoon of black pepper at this stage. This is traditionally a curry that is heavy in black pepper and you can add more to taste at the end of cooking. Stir in the chicken pieces followed by the green peppers, tomatoes and sliced red onion. Add the water or chicken stock and the soy sauce, if using, and cover the pan.

Cook over a medium heat for 5 minutes, then take off the lid and continue simmering or another 10 minutes or until the sauce thickens to your liking and the chicken is cooked through.

To finish, pour in the coconut milk and continue simmering to thicken. You can either serve this with a lot of sauce or reduce it down. Season with salt and perhaps a little more black pepper to taste.

GENERAL TSO'S CHICKEN

SERVES 4–6

General Tso's chicken is one of the most popular dishes at US Chinese restaurants, as it originated there. You are very unlikely to find it in China but the recipe is obviously greatly inspired by Chinese cooking, so I decided to feature it here. I just couldn't leave one of my favourite chicken dishes out of a chicken cookbook!

PREP TIME: 10 MINS
COOKING TIME: 20 MINS

700g (1lb 9oz) chicken thighs
  or breasts, cut into 2.5cm
  (1in) cubes
Rapeseed (canola) or peanut oil,
  for deep-frying

FOR THE MARINADE
2 medium egg whites
1½ tbsp Chinese rice wine
2 tbsp light soy sauce
1 tbsp cornflour (cornstarch)

FOR THE DRY COATING
120g (1 cup) plain (all-purpose)
  flour or rice flour (gluten-free)
120g (1 cup) cornflour
  (cornstarch)
1 level tsp baking powder
1 tsp sea salt

FOR THE SAUCE
4 tbsp Chinese rice wine or
  dry sherry
2 tbsp chicken stock or water
3 tbsp light soy sauce
1 tbsp dark soy sauce
1 tbsp ketchup (I use Heinz)
1 tbsp cornflour (cornstarch)
2 tbsp sugar, or to taste
2 tbsp rapeseed (canola) or
  peanut oil
2 tbsp minced garlic
1 tbsp minced ginger
3 tbsp thinly sliced spring
  onions (scallions)
8 dried red Chinese chillies
Zest of 1 small orange
1 tsp toasted sesame oil

TO GARNISH
3 spring onions (scallions),
  chopped into 2.5cm
  (1in) pieces
1 tbsp sesame seeds

Start by preparing the marinade. Whisk the egg whites in a mixing bowl until bubbly and then stir in the remaining marinade ingredients and whisk until smooth. Now add the chicken pieces and mix well with your hands to coat. Allow to marinate while you prepare the rest of the dish, or marinate overnight, covered, in the fridge for even better flavour.

To prepare the sauce, whisk the rice wine or sherry, chicken stock, soy sauces, ketchup, cornflour (cornstarch) and sugar together until smooth. Taste it and decide if you want to add more sugar. Set aside.

When ready to cook, heat about 750ml (3 cups) of rapeseed (canola) or peanut oil in a large wok. While the oil is heating up, mix the dry coating ingredients together in a bowl. When the oil reaches 180°C (350°F) you're ready to fry! Dip the marinated chicken pieces in the dry coating mixture to coat, in batches, and shake off any excess flour. Cook the chicken in small batches and be sure not to cook too many at once or the oil will cool and your chicken won't get crispy. Fry each batch for about 4 minutes or until lightly browned and crispy. Set aside on a rack to drip off any excess oil. Discard the cooking oil and wipe your wok clean.

Place the wok over a medium–high heat until a drop of water dissolves on contact. Now add the 2 tablespoons of rapeseed or peanut oil and swirl it around. Add the minced garlic, ginger, finely chopped spring onions (scallions), dried red chillies and orange zest and fry until fragrant. This should take about a minute. Stir in the prepared sauce and bring to a simmer. Continue cooking until the sauce has thickened slightly and then stir in the fried chicken. To finish, swirl in the toasted sesame oil and garnish with the chopped spring onions and sesame seeds to serve.

THAI CHICKEN BIRYANI
SERVES 4–6

Thai chicken biryani or Khao mok gai is one of the most popular rice dishes in Thailand. It isn't particularly spicy but is often served with a spicy sauce such as sriracha.

PREP TIME: 15 MINS
COOKING TIME: 40 MINS

1kg (2lb 2oz) chicken thighs
   and/or legs
4 tbsp rapeseed (canola) oil
1 medium onion, thinly sliced
2.5cm (1in) cinnamon stick
2 star anise
1 tsp each of black peppercorns
   and cloves
1 batch biryani paste (see below)
2 tbsp natural yoghurt
1 tsp garam masala (see page
   161) or curry powder
370g (2 cups) jasmine rice,
   rinsed
1 tsp salt
750ml (3 cups) homemade
   chicken stock (page 160)
   or water

FOR THE BIRYANI PASTE
5cm (2in) piece of ginger,
   roughly chopped
8 garlic cloves, smashed
4 large shallots, roughly chopped
1 bunch of coriander (cilantro),
   roughly chopped

FOR THE MARINADE
2 tbsp fish sauce
2 tbsp biryani paste (without the
   coriander/cilantro)
1 tsp ground turmeric
½ tsp garam masala (see
   page 161) or curry powder
3 tbsp natural yoghurt

Blend all of the biryani paste ingredients together, except the coriander (cilantro), until you have a fine or semi-fine paste. You can add a drop of water to assist blending if needed. Set aside. Place the chicken in a large mixing bowl and add the fish sauce, 2 tablespoons of the biryani paste, the turmeric, garam masala or curry powder and rub it all right into the flesh. Then stir in the yoghurt and ensure the chicken is completely coated with all these marinade ingredients. Allow to marinate while you prepare the rest of the dish or overnight. The longer, the better.

When ready to cook, add the coriander to the remaining biryani paste and blend until smooth. Set aside. You can add a little water to assist blending if needed. Heat the rapeseed (canola) oil over a medium–high heat in a high-sided frying pan (skillet) that has a lid. Add the sliced onion and fry for 10–15 minutes or until crispy and golden brown. Transfer the fried onion to a paper towel with a slotted spoon and set aside for later.

Now wipe as much of the marinade as you can off the chicken and add the chicken to the pan. Retain any leftover marinade. Fry it for about 4 minutes on each side until nicely caramelized on the exterior. It should be about 80 per cent cooked through. Transfer to a plate. There should still be sufficient oil in your pan, but if not, add a drop more. Stir in the cinnamon stick, star anise, black peppercorns and cloves and infuse their flavour into the oil for about 30 seconds. Pour in the prepared biryani paste and any retained marinade and fry it for a couple of minutes, stirring continuously. Then stir in the yoghurt along with the garam masala or curry powder.

Add the rinsed rice and salt and fry it for a couple of minutes with the paste. Pour in the chicken stock or water and return the fried chicken to the pan. Cover and simmer over a medium heat for about 20 minutes or until the rice has soaked up all the liquid and is cooked through.

Fluff up the rice with a fork or chopstick and serve immediately. This biryani is traditionally served with the cucumber salad on page 163. To serve, garnish the biryani with the fried onions and salad to taste.

CHICKEN HALEEM
SERVES 6

Go to a good and authentic Pakistani restaurant and you'll most likely see Haleem on the menu. When you see it, order it and you will see why I wanted to include Haleem in this book! Don't wait to try it out though. This recipe will get you authentic results and I'm quite sure you will want to make it again and again.

PREP TIME: 20 MINS, PLUS SOAKING
COOKING TIME: 2 HOURS

350g (2 cups) chana dal
200g (1 cup) red (masoor) dal
100g (½ cup) moong dal
100g (½ cup) white urad dal
170g (1 cup) cracked wheat
Salt, to taste
Lime wedges, to serve

FOR THE HALEEM
250ml (1 cup) ghee
2 large brown onions, thinly sliced
1kg (2lb 2oz) chicken thighs, on the bone and skinned
2 generous tbsp garlic and ginger paste

FOR THE HALEEM MASALA
1½ tbsp black peppercorns
4 black cardamoms, seeds only
4 green cardamoms, seeds only
1½ tbsp cumin seeds
1 tbsp coriander seeds
5 cloves
¼ nutmeg
1 blade mace
1 tsp fennel seeds
2.5cm (1in) cinnamon stick
1 star anise
1–2 tbsp Kashmiri chilli powder
1 tsp ground turmeric
250ml (1 cup) water

FOR THE TARKA
125ml (½ cup) ghee
5 tbsp julienned ginger
2–6 green finger chillies, thinly sliced

Wash and soak the dals and wheat for at least 3 hours or overnight. The longer you soak them, the faster your haleem will cook. Once soaked, pour the lentils and wheat into a large saucepan and cover with about 1.5 litres (6 cups) of water. Bring to a simmer over a medium–high heat. Lower the heat to medium and continue cooking for about 2 hours or until you can easily crush all the lentils and wheat between two fingers. You might need to add a little more water and be careful not to let the dal burn on the bottom of the pan.

Once cooked, add about 500ml (2 cups) water and blend it until creamy smooth, like pea soup. A stick blender will come in handy for this but the blending is optional. Heat the 250ml (1 cup) ghee in a large pan or wok over a medium–high heat. When visibly hot, add the sliced onions and fry for about 8 minutes or until golden brown. Transfer the fried onions to a paper towel to soak up any excess ghee. Add the chicken and fry, stirring regularly, for about 15 minutes or until the meat is beginning to fall off the bone. Transfer the chicken to a plate using a slotted spoon to cool some and then shred it with your hands or a fork. Discard the bones. Continue breaking the meat apart and shredding it until there are no big pieces. The smaller, the better.

Put this into the pot with the lentils and wheat and stir in the garlic and ginger paste. Simmer over a low–medium heat while you prepare the haleem masala. Pour all of the whole spices into a frying pan (skillet) and toast over a medium heat until warm to the touch and fragrant. Transfer to a plate to cool a little, then grind to a fine powder. Stir in the chilli powder and turmeric, then mix with the water. Stir to combine and then pour this into the simmering pot of chicken, lentils and wheat. Continue cooking the haleem until it is creamy and somewhat gooey. It should literally ooze off your spoon. I should stress again that you really want to stir regularly if not continuously so that the lentils don't scorch on the bottom. Season with salt to taste. I usually add about 2 tablespoons but how much is down to your personal preference.

To finish, heat the ghee for the tarka in a small pan. When bubbling hot, stir in the ginger and chillies and fry for a couple of minutes until the ginger is about one tone darker in colour. Pour about half over the haleem. The remaining tarka and the fried onions can be added to taste at the table. Serve with the lime wedges to squeeze over.

CHICKEN RENDANG
SERVES 4

Although beef rendang is by far the most famous, chicken rendang has gained popularity beyond its country of origin, Indonesia, specifically the West Sumatra region of the country. Its unique combination of spices and its depth of flavours make it a much sought-after dish, often served with steamed rice as part of a larger Indonesian or Malay meal or on its own.

PREP TIME: 15 MINS
COOKING TIME: 30 MINS

70ml (¼ cup) coconut or rapeseed (canola) oil
5cm (2in) cinnamon stick
2 star anise
4 cloves
4 cardamom pods, lightly bruised
2 lemongrass stalks, white parts only, thinly sliced
800g (1lb 12oz) boneless chicken thighs, skinned and cubed
400ml (1½ cups) thick tinned (canned) coconut milk
250ml (1 cup) water
5 makrut lime leaves, stemmed and thinly sliced
6 tbsp toasted fresh or frozen grated coconut (kerisik)★
1½ tsp tamarind paste
1 tsp palm sugar or light brown sugar, or more to taste
Salt, to taste

FOR THE RENDANG PASTE
6 shallots, roughly chopped
6 garlic cloves, smashed
2.5cm (1in) piece of galangal, peeled and roughly chopped
2 lime leaves, stemmed and roughly chopped
2 lemongrass stalks, white parts only, thinly sliced
12 dried red chillies, soaked in water for 20 minutes

TO GARNISH
2 red spur chillies, thinly sliced
3 spring onions (scallions), thinly sliced

For best results, place all the rendang paste ingredients in a pestle and mortar and pound to a paste. This could take up to 30 minutes, so you can use a food processor to speed things up, which is what I normally do. Set aside until ready to cook.

Heat the oil in a large clay pot, wok or frying pan (skillet) over a medium–high heat. When visibly hot and bubbly, stir in the whole spices and allow them to infuse into the oil for about 30 seconds. Then add the prepared rendang paste and fry for a further 30 seconds to cook out the rawness.

Add the thinly sliced lemongrass, followed by the chicken and stir well to combine. Fry for about 5 minutes or until the chicken is almost cooked through and then add the coconut milk and the water to cover.

Add the lime leaves and bring to a simmer. Stir in the toasted coconut (kerisik), tamarind and sugar, cover and cook over a medium heat for about 20 minutes or until the sauce has almost dried up and is coating the chicken pieces.

Check for seasoning, adding salt to taste and a little more sugar if desired, and serve garnished with the sliced red chillies and spring onions (scallions).

★ NOTE
Grated and toasted fresh or frozen coconut is called kerisik and it is available at many Southeast Asian specialty grocers. It's just toasted, grated coconut and you can make it easily at home. Place the grated coconut in a frying pan over a medium–high heat and toast it until lightly browned. It can be left grated or you could grind it into a paste with a drop of water. This really enhances the flavour of the rendang.

FRYING AND STIR-FRIES

Deep-frying and stir-frying chicken is one of my favourite ways to cook it. This is a collection of my six favourite fried dishes while writing this book. There were a lot of them but these simply had to feature.

CHICKEN CHAPLI KEBABS
SERVES 4

You could just cook these Chapli kebabs as you would any burger patty. That would work but a proper Chapli kebab needs to be deep-fried. As it fries, the meat turns a delicious brown and it becomes so crispy. These can be eaten as they are or stacked in burger buns with your salad veg and condiments of choice.

PREP TIME: 15 MINS, PLUS (OPTIONAL) MARINATING
COOKING TIME: 10 MINS

600g (1lb 5oz) minced (ground) chicken
2 red onions, roughly chopped
3–4 green bird's eye chillies
2.5cm (1in) piece of ginger, roughly chopped
5 garlic cloves, smashed and roughly chopped
2 tbsp gram (chickpea) flour
1 tsp salt
1 tsp freshly ground black pepper
1 tbsp coriander seeds
½ tsp ground turmeric
1 large tomato, thinly sliced
Rapeseed (canola) oil, for frying

Place the minced (ground) chicken in a large mixing bowl and add all the remaining ingredients, except for the sliced tomato and oil. Mix well with your hands so that everything is well combined. Leave to marinate for 8 hours or overnight or just carry on with the recipe. The longer marinating time will benefit the end dish.

When ready to cook, divide the chicken mixture into 8 equal-sized balls. They should all weigh about 75g (2½oz) each. Flatten the meatballs lightly with a spatula and press a slice of tomato or two into each patty. Then flatten some more to secure the tomato in the meat. Heat about 10cm (4in) rapeseed (canola) oil in a large wok or frying pan (skillet). The oil is hot enough to start cooking when thousands of little bubbles form immediately when you place a wooden spatula or chopstick in the oil.

Ease the patties into the oil and fry for about 6 minutes or until crispy and cooked through. Transfer the cooked patties to a plate lined with a paper towel to soak up any excess oil. Eat as they are with some hot sauce or a chutney or raita like those featured at the end of this book, or stack them into double burgers with salad veg, cheese and condiments of your choice.

CRISPY INDONESIAN FRIED CHICKEN
SERVES 4

You are going to love this flavoursome and crispy fried chicken. This recipe is right up there with the best of all the fried chicken I've eaten throughout my life. In fact, it could well be the best. This fried chicken is amazing served with a good hot sauce such as sambal oelek.

PREP TIME: 20 MINS,
PLUS MARINATING
COOKING TIME: 15 MINS

1kg (2lb 2oz) chicken thighs
   and legs on the bone
1 tsp salt
1 tsp ground black pepper
85g (⅓ cup) rice flour or
   cornflour (cornstarch)
Rapeseed (canola) oil,
   for deep-frying
Sat and pepper, to taste

FOR THE MARINADE
5 shallots, roughly chopped
5 garlic cloves, smashed
2.5cm (1in) piece of ginger,
   roughly chopped
2.5cm (1in) piece of galangal,
   roughly chopped
2 makrut lime leaves, stems
   removed and roughly chopped
1 tsp ground coriander
1 tsp ground cumin
1 tbsp ground turmeric
2 lemongrass stalks, white part
   only, finely chopped

Season the chicken with the salt and pepper. This can be done up to a day before you fry. To make the marinade, blend all the ingredients in a blender or food processor with just enough water to make a smooth marinade. Pour the marinade all over the chicken and add the flour. Mix well with your hands to coat. Allow to marinate for at least 30 minutes or up to 24 hours. The longer, the better.

When ready to fry, heat enough oil for deep-frying over a high heat. You are aiming for a cooking temperature of 175°C (345°F). If you don't have an oil thermometer, just check that the oil is hot enough to fry by carefully dipping one piece of chicken in. If thousands of little bubbles form and bubble around the chicken on contact, you're good to go. Depending on your pan, you might need to fry the chicken in small batches so that the oil retains this cooking heat. If the oil cools down, your chicken will become soggy instead of crispy.

Carefully add the chicken and fry for about 15 minutes or until golden brown and crispy. Be sure to move the chicken around in the pan from time to time so that it doesn't stick to the bottom. Transfer the cooked chicken to a metal rack to drip any excess oil and season with salt and pepper to taste.

CHICKEN JALI KEBABS
SERVES 2–4

Jali means 'net' so these are chicken net kebabs. They are fun to make and serve. The net is made by swirling beaten egg over the kebab as it cooks in hot oil. The kebabs look like they are encased in a net and they taste and look amazing.

PREP TIME: 15 MINS,
PLUS SITTING TIME
COOKING TIME: 10 MINS

6 tbsp rapeseed (canola) oil
1 medium red onion,
    thinly sliced
125ml (½ cup) milk
2 slices of white bread,
    crusts removed
450g (1lb) minced (ground)
    chicken
2 tbsp garlic and ginger paste
2–3 green bird's eye chillies,
    finely chopped
2 tsp Kashmiri chilli powder
2 tsp garam masala
    (see page 161)
2 tbsp mint leaves, finely
    chopped
2 tbsp coriander (cilantro),
    finely chopped
3 eggs, beaten
100g (1 cup) panko breadcrumbs
Salt and pepper, to taste

Heat the oil in a frying pan (skillet) or wok over a medium–high heat. When a small piece of onion sizzles and rises to the top on contact, stir in the sliced onion and fry for about 10–15 minutes, stirring often, until the onion is golden brown. Transfer to a mixing bowl with 1 tablespoon of the cooking oil. Pour the remaining cooking oil into a bowl, as you will need it for frying the kebabs.

Now pour the milk into a bowl and add the bread. Push the bread right down in the milk and then pick it up and squeeze out as much moisture as you can. Add this damp bread to the bowl with the onion and then add all the remaining ingredients, except for the eggs and the breadcrumbs. Mix well with your hands until well combined and then divide into 8 equal-sized patties. I recommend making them as neat as you can for better presentation.

Pour the retained oil from the fried onions into a high-sided pan and then pour in more oil until the oil in your pan is deep enough to deep-fry the patties. Usually just 5cm (2in) of oil will suffice. Place the oil over a medium–high heat. It is hot enough to start frying when you stick a wooden chopstick or spatula in and thousands of little bubbles form instantly around the wood.

With practice, the next step can be done by cooking all of the kebabs at once, but I recommend starting with one to get the idea about how these kebabs should cook and look when finished. Dip one of the kebabs in the beaten eggs and then coat it completely with the breadcrumbs. Add the kebab to the oil and fry for about 3 minutes or until crispy brown and cooked through. Take a spoonful of the beaten eggs and swirl it in a thin stream over the kebab in a circular motion. This will form the 'net'. Flip it over and do the same thing on the other side and then flip it over again and transfer the cooked kebab to a wire rack to drip any excess oil. Repeat with the remaining kebabs.

Season with salt and pepper to taste and serve with hot sauce, chutney or raita.

KOREAN MISO CHICKEN
SERVES 4

Japanese miso chicken has always been a favourite at our house. This Korean version is similar but spicier, so I like it even more. Some chefs add a little sugar but the gochujang is sweet enough for my liking. You can add more sugar to taste though, if you prefer a sweeter flavour.

PREP TIME: 10 MINS
COOKING TIME: 30 MINS

5 tbsp white miso
5 tbsp gochujang (Korean hot
    pepper paste)
3 tbsp toasted sesame oil
2 tbsp rice wine vinegar
1 tbsp soy sauce
1 tsp freshly ground
    black pepper
1kg (2lb 2oz) chicken thighs,
    cut into bite-sized pieces
200g (7oz) long-stem broccoli,
    roughly chopped at an angle
4 garlic cloves, finely chopped
2.5cm (1in) piece of ginger,
    finely chopped
4 spring onions (scallions),
    thinly sliced
1 tsp gochugaru (Korean hot
    pepper flakes)

Place the miso, gochujang, 1 tablespoon of the sesame oil, the rice vinegar, soy sauce and black pepper in a large mixing bowl and whisk until smooth. Transfer half of the marinade to another bowl and set aside for later. Add the chicken to the remaining marinade and rub the marinade right into the flesh. Allow to marinate for 30 minutes or up to 2 hours.

When ready to cook, bring enough water to cover the broccoli to the boil in a saucepan. Add the broccoli and simmer for 4 minutes. The broccoli should still be a bit undercooked. Strain and set aside.

Heat the remaining sesame oil in a wok. When smoking hot, add the garlic, ginger and half of the spring onions (scallions) to the wok and fry for about 30 seconds or until fragrant. Add the marinated chicken and fry, stirring and tossing your wok, until lightly charred and cooked through. This should take about 5 minutes. Add the par-cooked broccoli and fry for another couple of minutes or until cooked to your liking. Pour in the remaining marinade and fry until hot. Sprinkle in the gochugaru and serve over white rice garnished with the remaining spring onions (scallions).

KOLKATA CHICKEN CHAAP
SERVES 4

Chicken chaap is a dish that is served in two ways. You could just dust the marinated chicken with the flours and fry it in some oil. That is Chicken chaap. The popular street-food version is a bit more work. The chicken is first fried and then torn or chopped up with a knife or spatula. It's then stir-fried with vegetables before adding a mouthwatering, zingy sauce. That's what you're getting here!

PREP TIME: 25 MINS
COOKING TIME: 25 MINS

8 large boneless, skinless
   chicken thighs
250ml (1 cup) rapeseed (canola)
   oil, for shallow-frying
120g (1 cup) gram (chickpea)
   flour
60g (½ cup) cornflour
   (cornstarch) or rice flour
1 red onion, thinly sliced
1 red (bell) pepper and 1 yellow
   (bell) pepper, seeded and
   thinly sliced
3–4 green finger chillies,
   thinly sliced
2 medium tomatoes, diced

FOR THE MARINADE
3 tbsp garlic and ginger paste
1 tbsp Dijon mustard
2 tbsp lime juice
1 tsp mustard or rapeseed
   (canola) oil
1 tsp ground cumin
2 tsp ground coriander
1–2 tbsp Kashmiri chilli powder
1 tsp garam masala
   (see page 161)
1 tsp ground black pepper
4 tbsp Greek yoghurt

FOR THE SAUCE
1 red onion, roughly chopped
4 garlic cloves
2.5cm (1in) piece of ginger,
   roughly chopped
2 green bird's eye chillies,
   roughly chopped
4 tbsp mustard oil or rapeseed
   (canola) oil
1 tbsp rice wine or cider vinegar
3 tbsp ketchup
2 tbsp light soy sauce or tamari
2 tbsp oyster sauce

Start by whisking the marinade ingredients together in a mixing bowl. Set aside. Place the chicken thighs on a large piece of cling film (plastic wrap) on your countertop and top with another piece of cling film. Pound with a meat mallet or something else suitable until the thighs have doubled in size and are quite thin. Place the pounded thighs in the marinade and cover. Marinate the chicken for 30 minutes or up to 24 hours. If in a rush, you could just start cooking but the longer you can marinate the chicken, the better.

Now prepare the sauce. It's too good! Blend the onion, garlic, ginger and chillies with just enough water to make a thick paste. Heat the mustard or rapeseed (canola) oil over a medium–high heat, add the paste and fry for about 3 minutes. Then add the vinegar, ketchup, soy sauce and oyster sauce. Simmer for about 5 minutes or until the sauce has reduced by about half. Set aside.

To finish, heat the rapeseed (canola) oil for shallow-frying in a pan over a high heat. Your oil is ready for frying when you stick a wooden spatula or chopstick in and thousands of little bubbles form around it on contact.

Pour the flours onto a plate and mix well to combine. Then scrape off any excess marinade from the chicken and place the chicken in the flour to coat. Shake off any excess flour and place the chicken in the hot oil to fry. When your chicken pieces are turning golden brown on the bottom, flip them over to fry the other side for a few minutes. The thinly pounded chicken should cook through quite quickly. Transfer the crispy fried chicken to a clean surface and cut into bite-sized pieces.

Now add about 3 tablespoons of the oil you used to fry the chicken to a pan over a medium–high heat. When a small piece of onion sizzles and rises to the top on contact, add the thinly sliced onion, (bell) peppers, chillies and tomatoes and stir-fry for about 3 minutes. Then add the chicken and stir it all up to combine. Add the sauce. You might not want to add it all, but you can if you like a lot of sauce. Continue frying until the chicken is hot and serve with chapattis, naans or parathas.

CHICKEN SHAMI KEBABS

SERVES 2, OR 4 AS A STARTER OR SIDE DISH

The goal with these amazing chicken shami kebabs is to get the exterior a crispy, deep golden brown with a soft, somewhat stringy texture in the centre. Just follow this recipe and you will be in shami kebab heaven. You could just serve them with quartered limes, which you squeeze over the kebabs at the table, but I like to serve them with the sliced onions and the green chilli and coriander chutney on page 169, which I had them with on several occasions in Delhi.

PREP TIME: 15 MINS
COOKING TIME: 1 HOUR

200g (1 cup) split chana lentils, washed and soaked in water for at least 30 minutes
600g (1lb 5oz) boneless chicken thighs, cut into 3 pieces each
6 garlic cloves, roughly chopped
1 level tsp fine sea salt
½ tsp cumin seeds
½ tsp coriander seeds, lightly crushed
6 dried Kashmiri chillies, roughly chopped
Approx.1 litre (4 cups) water
2 eggs
1 medium onion, grated and squeezed of excess moisture
2 tbsp coriander (cilantro) leaves, finely chopped
1½ tsp Kashmiri chilli powder
1 tsp garam masala (see page 161)
Rapeseed (canola) oil, for shallow-frying

TO SERVE
2 limes, quartered
Green chilli and coriander chutney (see page 169)
1 white or red onion, thinly sliced

Get your split chana lentils on to soak while you prepare the rest of the dish. You could soak them for a couple of hours if convenient, as this will speed up the cooking process. Place the chicken, garlic, salt, cumin and coriander seeds and the dried Kashmiri chillies in a saucepan and pour 250ml (1 cup) of the water over it all. Bring to a simmer over a medium–high heat, cover the pan and allow to simmer for about 20 minutes or until the chicken is cooked through and becoming tender.

Strain the soaked chana lentils and add them to the pan. Add another 500ml (2 cups) of the water. Bring back to a simmer, cover and continue simmering for 30 minutes or until all the water has evaporated and the lentils are so soft you can smash them between two fingers. You may need to add more water to cook the lentils so keep an eye on them. By this time, you should easily be able to break up the chicken pieces with a wooden spatula. Take off the heat.

Begin smashing the ingredients in the pan with a wooden spatula or potato masher. You want to spend some time doing this as you need to ensure all the lentils are 90 per cent smashed and the ingredients are well combined. Add the eggs, the grated, squeezed onion, coriander (cilantro), chilli powder and garam masala and continue mashing it all together until the mixture looks like clay when squeezed into a ball but the chicken still looks quite stringy.

Divide the mashed chicken mixture into four equal-sized balls. Then form the balls into neat, flattened patties. If you want to get really posh with this, use a metal ring mould to ensure they all look the same.

Now heat about 5cm (2in) of oil in a frying pan (skillet). When visibly hot, carefully add the shami kebabs and fry on one side until crispy, brown and lightly caramelized and then flip them over to do the same to the other side. Transfer the cooked shami kebabs to a wire rack to drip any excess oil. Serve hot with lime wedges or the green chilli and coriander chutney and sliced onions.

WRAPS AND SANDWICHES

Looking for a great sandwich to hold you over until dinner? Or perhaps you want that sandwich or wrap to be dinner. You can serve these sandwiches as you like, either as a quick snack or as a big party meal.

These are all quite easy to prepare,
so why not try thcm all?

BÁNH MÌ
SERVES 4

Hoi An is one of the most beautiful cities in the world. We stayed for a week but could easily have extended our stay for months. I loved trying all the different dishes and seeing the area. One of the things I ordered often for lunch in Vietnam was a good bánh mì and in Hoi An you'll find the best, with all kinds of delicious fillings. The top places would always spread a good helping of chicken or pork pâté over the bottom piece of bread. These are really just a Vietnamese version of a subway sandwich but with their own, French-influenced touch, and any cold cuts can be added. The carrot and radish salad is simply a must for any bánh mì. If you want to get really fancy with this chicken version, be sure to add some of the chicken floss from page 162. I have also featured a few other optional toppings and I like to pile them high on my bánh mìs!

PREP TIME: 15 MINS, PLUS MARINATING
COOKING TIME: 15 MINS

4 fresh French baguettes, sliced
225g (8oz) chunky chicken pâté or another good-quality pâté
700g (1lb 9oz) chicken cold cuts or pieces of the Vietnamese roast chicken (see page 143)

FOR THE CARROT AND RADISH PICKLE
125ml (½ cup) white distilled vinegar
125ml (½ cup) water
4 generous tbsp white sugar
1 tsp salt
2 large carrots, peeled and julienned (approx. 225g/8oz)
1 mooli radish (daikon), peeled and julienned (approx. 225g/8oz)

OPTIONAL TOPPINGS
The Laughing Cow cheese
1 cucumber, thinly sliced
2 tomatoes, thinly sliced
1–2 heads baby gem lettuce, shredded
3 spring onions (scallions), thinly sliced
2–3 red spur chillies, thinly sliced
20 pickled jalapeños
8 tbsp coriander (cilantro), finely chopped
8 tbsp mayonnaise
2 tbsp sriracha sauce
8 tbsp chicken floss (see page 162)

To make the carrot and radish (daikon) pickle, heat the vinegar and water in a pan over a medium–high heat and add the sugar and salt. As the liquid comes to a simmer, the sugar and salt will dissolve. Turn off the heat and allow to cool a little.

Pour the cooled liquid over the julienned carrots and radish. For best results, allow this to pickle for a day or more in a sterile jar, covered, in the fridge. You can use it the same day though. Depending on how big of a fan of carrot and radish pickle you are, you might have some left over.

To build the bánh mì, cover the bottom piece of bread with a generous helping of pâté. You can then add chicken cold cuts or anything really. I like to add leftover Vietnamese roast chicken but any cold cuts will do here. Stack it high with the carrot and radish pickle, The Laughing Cow cheese and the optional veggies, chillies and herbs of your choice, then top with mayonnaise and sriracha. I really like to add chicken floss to my bánh mìs. If you don't mind a little work, you can make it at home following my recipe on page 162. You can purchase chicken floss online and at specialty shops though.

NOTE
The Vietnamese are not big cheese eaters but the mild French, The Laughing Cow processed cheese is a popular topping.

TANDOORI CHICKEN BURGER
SERVES 4

This is a mega burger with a difference! The fried tandoori chicken is so crispy and tasty. Together with the other ingredients, you will find it hard to find a better chicken burger, I promise.

PREP TIME: 20 MINS
COOKING TIME: 20 MINS

2 large chicken breasts or more
   if needed (about 1kg/2lb 2oz),
   skin on or off
1 litre (4 cups) rapeseed
   (canola) oil
Green chilli and coriander
   chutney (see page 169)
4 burger buns, halved and
   toasted in a little butter

FOR THE MARINADE
Juice of 1 lemon
2 tbsp garlic and ginger paste
2 tbsp mustard oil or rapeseed
   (canola) oil (I use mustard oil)
1 tbsp, Kashmiri chilli powder
   (more or less to taste)
1 tbsp paprika
1 tbsp tandoori masala
1 tbsp ground cumin
1 tbsp ground coriander
3 generous tbsp thick full-fat
   yoghurt (optional)
Salt, to taste

FOR THE BATTER COATING
3 large eggs
250ml (1 cup) sparkling water
   (club soda)
600g (3 cups) plain (all-purpose)
   flour
1 tbsp each of Kashmiri chilli
   powder, paprika, ground
   cumin, ground coriander
   and tandoori masala
1 tbsp salt
1 tbsp ground black pepper

FOR THE SPRING
ONION RAITA
210g (1 cup) Greek yoghurt
2 garlic cloves, minced
4 spring onions (scallions),
   finely chopped
Juice of 1–2 limes
Salt, to taste
Milk (optional)

Begin by preparing the spring onion raita. Whisk all the ingredients up to and including the spring onions (scallions) together. Then add lime juice and salt to taste. If this isn't thin enough for you, stir in a little milk to thin some more. Cover and place in the fridge until ready to use.

Place the chicken breasts on a clean work surface and slice lengthwise through the centre, then cut each piece in half. Put the chicken in a large mixing bowl and add the lemon juice, 1 teaspoon of salt and the garlic and ginger paste and mix well with your hands until equally coated. Set aside while you make the rest of the marinade.

In another bowl, mix the oil with the chilli powder, paprika, tandoori masala and ground cumin and coriander. If not taking the time to marinate the chicken, don't add the yoghurt. Otherwise, whisk in the yoghurt and mix this all in with the chicken. If you added yoghurt, allow to marinate for at least 3 hours or up to 48 hours. The longer, the better. Do not allow chicken without the yoghurt to marinate for more than 2 hours.

When ready to cook, whisk the eggs and sparkling water (club soda) together with 200g (1 cup) of the flour until you have a creamy smooth batter. Pour the remaining flour onto a large plate and stir in the chilli powder, paprika, ground cumin and coriander, tandoori masala, salt and pepper. Remove the chicken from the marinade and shake off any excess. Dip it into the flour mixture and then into the batter. Shake off any excess batter. Then roll each piece in the seasoned flour again and shake off any excess flour.

Heat the rapeseed (canola) oil until it reaches 175°C (350°F). When ready, slowly lower the chicken into the hot oil. You should cook in two batches so that the oil retains its heat. Fry each batch for 7–8 minutes or until you have an internal temperature of 75°C (165°F). Keep the cooked chicken warm while you cook the second batch.

To build the burgers, spread some of the green chilli and coriander chutney over the bottom buns. Add sliced onions, cheese slices, pickled jalapeños, sliced tomato and lettuce as you wish, then stack a couple of pieces of chicken on top. Pour over some of the spring onion raita and more green chilli and coriander chutney to taste and place the top bun on top of it all. Serve immediately.

CHICKEN SHAMI BUN KEBABS

SERVES 4

Chicken sandwiches are, of course, something you can make on a whim without any recipe. Here I take the classic bun kebab which is normally made with vegetarian shami kebabs and use my chicken shami kebabs instead. So you will need to first prepare the shami kebab mixture on page 111, but the cooking method to complete this dish is different. So don't fry that chicken shami mixture as in the shami kebab recipe. Instead, do this! You'll love every bite.

PREP TIME: 10 MINS, PLUS MAKING THE CHICKEN SHAMI MIXTURE
COOKING TIME: 15 MINS

1 batch chicken shami kebab mixture (see page 111)
2–4 tbsp butter
4 burger buns, sliced through the middle
Rapeseed (canola) oil, for shallow-frying
4 eggs
6 tbsp (¼ cup) mayonnaise
6 tbsp sriracha or your hot sauce of choice
2 red onions, thinly sliced
1 green (bell) pepper or ¼ cucumber, thinly sliced
3 medium tomatoes, thinly sliced
½ iceberg lettuce, shredded
Pickled jalapeño chillies (as many as you like)
4 burger cheese slices or the equivalent of shredded paneer (optional)

FOR THE GREEN SAUCE
60g (2oz) coriander (cilantro), roughly chopped
20 mint leaves
Juice of 1 lemon or lime (to taste)
1 tsp salt, or to taste
1 tsp ground cumin
6 green finger chillies, roughly chopped
2 garlic cloves, roughly chopped
70ml (¼ cup) Green yoghurt

Place the coriander (cilantro), mint leaves, lemon juice, salt, cumin, green chillies and garlic in a blender and blend with just enough water to make a thick paste. Pour this into a bowl and start whisking in the yoghurt. For a thicker sauce, just add about 2 tablespoons of yoghurt or you could add it all for a creamier sauce. Set aside.

Divide the chicken shami kebab mixture into four equal-sized patties and set aside. Now add 2 tablespoons of the butter to a large, high-sided frying pan (skillet) over a medium–high heat. Add the burger buns, sliced side down, and fry them for a couple of minutes until they are a toasty, golden brown. Add more butter if needed.

Remove the toasted buns from the pan and add about 10cm (4in) rapeseed (canola) oil and bring to about 175°C (350°F). If you don't have an oil thermometer, you can stick the handle of a wooden spatula or a wooden chopstick in the oil. When thousands of little bubbles form around the wood on contact, your oil is ready for frying.

Beat the eggs until creamy smooth in a large mixing bowl. Coat the shami kebabs in the beaten eggs and then slowly lower them into the hot oil. Fry for a few minutes or until crispy and golden, then transfer the kebabs to a wire rack to drip any excess oil.

To finish these bun kebabs off, spread the green sauce, mayonnaise and hot sauce over the browned sides of the buns. Layer the bottom buns with the sliced vegetables and chillies and then top each with a shami kebab and the cheese, if using.

Your bun kebabs can now be served, or if you prefer, you could place them back in a pan to toast the top of the buns and melt the cheese, if using.

CHICKEN FRANKIE
SERVES 4

If you live near an Indian grocer, you could purchase parathas in the frozen section. Frankies are wraps that are normally made using homemade parathas at street-food stalls, but here I have simplified the recipe to use tortillas. The result tastes amazingly just like those you find in India but without all the hard work of making your own parathas. This is food to be eaten on the go! You pack as much chicken and veggies in the wrap as you can, then tightly roll it up and wrap the frankie tightly in foil to reduce spillage. The chicken is usually slathered with a good chutney or two such as green chilli and coriander chutney (page 169) and tamarind sauce.

PREP TIME: 15 MINS, PLUS (OPTIONAL) MARINATING
COOKING TIME: 30 MINS

450g (1lb) chicken breast or thigh meat, thinly sliced against the grain
2 tbsp rapeseed (canola) oil
2 medium red onions, thinly sliced and cut into 2.5cm (1in) pieces
2 tbsp garlic and ginger paste
2–3 green bird's eye chillies, thinly sliced or left whole
1 tsp each of ground turmeric, ground cumin, ground coriander, amchoor (dried mango powder), anardana (pomegranate powder) and chaat masala
1 tsp Kashmiri chilli powder, plus extra to taste if you like it spicy
125ml (½ cup) water
3 tbsp chopped coriander (cilantro)
Salt, to taste
Chutneys of your choice, to serve

FOR THE MARINADE
2 tbsp garlic and ginger paste
1 tsp salt
1 tsp freshly ground black pepper
1 tbsp lemon juice

FOR THE WRAPS
4 tbsp ghee or rapeseed (canola) oil
4 large tortillas
4 eggs, beaten

Place the sliced chicken in a bowl with all the marinade ingredients. Stir well to combine and allow to marinate for 30 minutes or up to 2 hours. It you're in a rush, you could just go straight to cooking.

When ready to cook, heat the oil in a large frying pan (skillet) over a medium–high heat. When small bubbles begin to form, stir in the sliced red onions and fry for about 7 minutes or until soft, translucent and lightly browned. Stir in the garlic and ginger paste along with the chopped or whole chillies and then add the ground spices.

Give this all a good stir and then add the marinated chicken and stir some more until the chicken is completely coated with the sauce. Continue frying until the chicken begins to turn white on the exterior and then add the water and chopped coriander (cilantro). Cover the pan and cook over a medium heat for 10 minutes. Give it all a good stir and then continue cooking, covered, for another 10 minutes. Taste it and add more salt if needed. Take the lid off the pan and carry on simmering until almost all of the liquid has evaporated but the chicken is still looking nice and juicy. Set aside and keep warm.

To save time, you could prepare the tortillas while the chicken is simmering. I recommend using a non-stick pan if you have one. Heat a quarter of the ghee or oil in your pan over a medium–high heat. When hot, add one of the tortillas and let it lightly brown for about a minute. Then flip it over to brown the other side. The tortilla should puff up as it cooks, which is normal. Transfer the fried tortilla to a plate and repeat with the remaining oil and tortillas. Keep warm.

Now add a quarter of the beaten eggs to the pan and roll it all around in the pan to make it as thin as you can. You can swirl it onto the sides of some pans, which will make it paper thin, though this is not necessary. The thin layer of egg will cook quickly, so top it with one of the fried tortillas and cook for about 20 seconds, then flip the egg-lined tortilla onto a plate and keep warm. Repeat with the remaining eggs and tortillas.

Place one of the egg-lined tortillas on a clean surface and top it with some chicken. You could also add sliced onion or other veggies. Add your chutneys of choice and then fold the top over before rolling it all up. Repeat with the remaining tortillas and chicken and serve hot or at room temperature. Hot is best!

KEEMA PAV
SERVES 4–6

Keema pav is a street-food favourite and this chicken keema pav is one of the best! You could, of course, use minced (ground) beef or lamb in this recipe too. The keema is so good and the oil that floats on top isn't bad either. This is real comfort food and a great way to serve the family. It's filling and also inexpensive to make.

PREP TIME: 15 MINS
COOKING TIME: 30 MINS

500g (1lb 2oz) minced (ground) chicken
4 tbsp lightly salted butter
4–6 fresh burger buns, sliced

FOR THE CURRY
3 tbsp mustard oil or rapeseed (canola) oil (I use mustard oil)
2 Indian bay leaves (cassia leaves)
5cm (2in) cinnamon stick
2 green cardamom pods or 1 black, bruised
5 cloves
1 tsp black peppercorns
3 medium red onions, very finely chopped
2 tbsp garlic and ginger paste
1 tbsp Kashmiri chilli powder (more or less to taste)
1 tsp garam masala (see page 161)
1 tsp ground fennel
Pinch of ground mace
1½ tbsp ground coriander
1 tbsp ground cumin
¾ tsp ground turmeric
125ml (½ cup) unseasoned passata
5 tbsp natural yoghurt, whisked until smooth
About 250ml (1 cup) water or chicken stock
4 green finger chillies, finely chopped
1 tbsp cold butter
3 tbsp coriander (cilantro), finely chopped
Salt, to taste

Heat the oil in a frying pan (skillet) over a medium–high heat until visibly hot. Stir the whole spices into the oil for about 30 seconds to flavour the oil. Add the chopped onions and fry for about 5 minutes or until soft and translucent. Add the garlic and ginger paste and stir it into the onions for about 30 seconds.

Mix the chilli powder, garam masala, fennel, mace, ground coriander, cumin and turmeric together and pour them into the pan, followed immediately with 70ml (¼ cup) of water and bring it all to a simmer. Stir in the passata and bring to a simmer. Reduce the heat to medium, cover and simmer for 5 minutes.

Lift the lid and add the minced (ground) chicken. Stir it right in with a wooden spoon or spatula and press it down to break up the meat for a couple of minutes until you have no lumps in the meat. Cover the pan again and cook for 5 minutes. When you lift the lid, you will see that the oil has risen to the top. Stir in the whisked yoghurt, 1 tablespoon at a time, until completely combined into the meat. Cover the pan again and cook for about 3 minutes.

Lift the lid and again you will see the oil floating on top and it will smell amazing. Pour in the water or stock and bring to a simmer over a medium–high heat. Let it simmer until it looks a bit like a Bolognese. Stir in the chopped chillies and cold butter and then try some and add salt to taste. Garnish with the chopped coriander. Keep warm.

Now, in another frying pan, melt 2 tablespoons of the salted butter over a medium–high heat and add half the buns. Toast on both sides in the hot butter and then repeat with the remaining butter and buns. Obviously, if you have a large enough pan, this can all be done at the same time.

Serve the keema either in a bowl and dip the buns in it or slather it all over the buns and dig in.

BARBECUE

In this chapter you'll find a delicious selection of recipes that are best cooked outdoors. For that matter, and this is my opinion, all of the recipes in this book are better cooked over fire, but perhaps that's just me.

It's worth noting that these recipes can all be cooked indoors too. Recipes that are cooked on the grill over hot coals can, of course, be fried. Those that are roasted can be cooked in your oven at the same temperature.

These are all new recipes, so you won't find Tandoori chicken tikka in this chapter. Recipes for that are in my previous books. I know some of you might want to do just that though, so I have featured my all-purpose tandoori marinade (see page 168), which will work on chicken and other meats, as well as paneer and vegetables.

SETTING UP YOUR BARBECUE

Unlike my book *The Curry Guy BBQ,* where six different cooking techniques are used, in this book you only need to think about two: direct heat cooking and indirect heat cooking. Here I would like to briefly cover what you need to know to get that barbecue producing delicious food for you.

LIGHTING YOUR FIRE

Like most people, I used to just squirt a large amount of liquid fire starter onto my charcoal and then throw a lit match at it, happily standing back to watch it burst into flames. You don't want to do that. You will taste that fire starter in your food, not to mention that it's quite dangerous. These days I light my fire using the following two methods.

THE STACK

Anyone who has lit a campfire or indoor fireplace will be familiar with this method. To do it, you will need some way of getting the fire going. Scrunch up some newspaper and place a bit of kindling wood on top and light it. You could also use a natural fire starter or two. Then, stack more kindling and lumpwood charcoal, kiln-dried logs or charcoal briquettes on top, ensuring that everything is loosely stacked into a pyramid shape to allow air to flow upwards and keep the fire going. From experience, you will need to allow yourself a good 30 minutes to get the fire ready for cooking.

CHIMNEY STARTER

Chimney starters are available online and at most shops that sell barbecues. A chimney starter reduces the fuss of building a good fire; it is a metal cylinder that has a large space at the top for loading your charcoal and a smaller space at the bottom that you fill with crunched up newspaper and natural fire starters. Light the bottom and let the chimney do its job. In about 20–30 minutes, you will have a full chimney of lit charcoal ready to use. However, you'll still need to decide how much charcoal you need and how to arrange it for the job in hand.

WHICH FUEL TO USE AND HOW MUCH?

I think of the charcoal and wood that I use for cooking as ingredients in their own right. Good-quality lumpwood charcoal, compressed briquettes and/or kiln-dried wood can add delicious flavour to your food, while poor-quality charcoal will do the opposite. For the recipes in this book, I used good-quality lumpwood charcoal for my direct heat cooking, as it gets good and hot. I used compressed charcoal for indirect cooking as it burns longer.

PREPARING THE BARBECUE FOR DIRECT HEAT GRILLING

Cooking over open flames is the simplest of the two methods used. When food is exposed to intense direct heat, it gets a wonderful, smoky char on the exterior, while the interior remains deliciously juicy.

When preparing the charcoal, it is a good idea to build a two-level fire. For ease, use a barbecue chimney starter to light the coals (see opposite). When the coals are white-hot, pour the charcoal into the basin of the barbecue, then spread the charcoal so that two-thirds of the coals are stacked about twice as high as the remaining one-third. This way, you can easily move whatever it is you are cooking from the hot side of the grill to the cooler side if it begins to burn before it's cooked through.

I use a lot of charcoal – about two full shoe boxes★ – as it is important to achieve that intense heat. To check if the coals are ready, hold your hand about 5cm (2in) above the cooking grate. If your hand becomes uncomfortably hot in 2 seconds, you're ready to start cooking.

PREPARING THE BARBECUE FOR INDIRECT COOKING

This method is used for roasting and you will need a barbecue that has a tight-fitting lid. Fill the barbecue on one side only with about two shoe boxes full of charcoal★, leaving the other half empty. Light a few natural firelighters and pile in the charcoal. Let it heat until white-hot, then place the grill on top and whatever it is you are cooking over the side with no coals. Cover and cook. If you are barbecuing for a long period of time, you will need to throw a few handfuls of charcoal on the fire every 30 minutes or so.

OVEN COOKING

Ovens vary, but I usually crank mine up to 200°C (400°F/Gas 6) and cook the meat on a wire rack near the top. To get that charred appearance and flavour, place the roasted meat under a hot grill (broiler) for about 2 minutes after cooking, just before serving.

★ The amount of charcoal you use depends on the size of your barbecue. Refer to your owner's manual for the manufacturer's recommendations.

CHICKEN BULGOGI
SERVES 4

Quite possibly the perfect grilled chicken! This one is so easy to prepare and can all be cooked over direct heat. It's sweet, spicy and savoury. I love the flavour of the charred chicken with all that Korean-style marinade. You can serve this over rice with a little soy sauce or soy sauce mixed with more gochugaru (Korean hot pepper flakes). If you like, you could double the marinade ingredients. Use half for marinating the chicken and the rest as a delicious dipping sauce.

PREP TIME: 10 MINS
COOKING TIME: 15 MINS

8 large boneless chicken thighs, skinned
3 tbsp gochujang (Korean hot pepper paste)
1½ tbsp gochugaru (Korean hot pepper flakes)
1 tbsp light brown sugar
1½ tbsp light soy sauce or tamari, plus extra to serve
2 tbsp garlic and ginger paste
1 tsp freshly ground black pepper
2 tbsp mirin
1½ tbsp sesame oil
Oil, for greasing
2 tbsp sesame seeds, toasted

Place the chicken thighs on a clean work surface and pound with a meat mallet to flatten slightly and tenderize. Put this chicken in a mixing bowl and add all the remaining ingredients, except the sesame seeds. Mix well with a spoon or your hands until the chicken is nicely coated. You can go straight to cooking or let the chicken marinate for a few hours or up to 24 hours. The longer, the better.

When ready to cook, build a direct heat fire in your barbecue (see page 127). The coals are ready when it becomes uncomfortably hot to hold your hand 5cm (2in) above cooking height for longer than 2 seconds.

Lightly grease the grilling surface with oil or kitchen oil spray and place the chicken on top. Cook for about 6 minutes or until the chicken is beginning to char on the underside. Flip the chicken over and cook the other side for 6 minutes, basting from time to time with any remaining marinade. Check for doneness and continue cooking until the chicken is completely cooked through.

Transfer to a cutting board and let it rest for 5 minutes. Then slice the chicken thinly against the grain. Serve the chicken, garnished with sesame seeds, over rice with soy sauce.

GRILLED BUTTER CHICKEN

SERVES 4–6

Unless you've been to the original Aslam Chicken in Chandni Chowk, Delhi, or one of their other new outlets, you probably haven't tried butter chicken like this before. The restaurant is now famous for their butter chicken and it really is so good! Large bowls of tandoori chicken are delivered to your table smothered in butter, yoghurt and spices, and it is meant to be shared among friends. The butter chicken is served with rumali rotis, which are paper thin rotis. You can purchase frozen rumali rotis at Indian grocers or serve your butter chicken with chapattis or naans. I have included a homemade rumali roti recipe on page 166. You pick up a piece of the buttery chicken with the roti and there are seriously very few food experiences that are so incredible! This isn't their exact Aslam Chicken recipe but it's close enough. At Aslam Chicken, the tandoori chicken thighs and legs are served in small pieces on the bone, but you could go boneless if you prefer.

PREP TIME: 10 MINS,
PLUS MARINATING
COOKING TIME: 20 MINS

1kg (2lb 2oz) bone-in or boneless
  chicken thighs, skin removed
  and cut into bite-sized pieces

FOR THE FIRST MARINADE
3 tbsp lemon juice
1 tsp salt
2 tbsp garlic and ginger paste
1 tsp rapeseed (canola) oil

FOR THE SECOND
MARINADE
70g (¼ cup) Greek yoghurt
1–3 tbsp Kashmiri chilli powder
  (to taste)
1 tbsp ground cumin
1 tbsp ground coriander
1 tsp amchoor powder
1 tbsp tandoori masala
1 tbsp garam masala
  (see page 161)
1 tsp ground turmeric
1 tsp ground black pepper
2 tbsp garlic, ginger and chilli
  paste (see page 161)

TO FINISH
250g (9oz) lightly salted butter
1 tbsp tandoori masala
4 tbsp Greek yoghurt
Flaky salt, to taste

Place the chicken pieces in a large mixing bowl. Add the lemon juice, salt, garlic and ginger paste and oil and rub it right into the flesh. Set aside while you prepare the second marinade.

In another bowl, whisk all of the second marinade ingredients together until smooth. Pour this marinade over the chicken and, again, rub it right into the flesh of the chicken. You can go straight to cooking now, but for best results, allow the chicken to marinate for at least 30 minutes. One or even two days of marinating will be even better.

When ready to cook, heat sufficient coals in your barbecue. Your coals are ready for cooking when it is uncomfortably hot for you to hold your hand 5cm (2in) above cooking height for longer than 2 seconds.

Skewer the chicken onto metal skewers by weaving the skewer through the chicken pieces. Don't just stick the skewer through or your chicken won't be properly secured on the skewers.

Place the chicken skewers over the fire. While the chicken is cooking, melt the butter over the coals in a small pan. Continue cooking and turning the skewers from time to time so that the chicken cooks evenly.

Once your chicken is cooked through and nicely charred, pour it into a serving bowl. Add half of the tandoori masala to the chicken pieces and mix it in. Add the remaining tandoori masala to the yoghurt and whisk to combine. Finally, pour the hot butter over the chicken and again stir it in before garnishing with some of the yoghurt. This should only be lightly stirred and tossed so that you see clear butter and yoghurt on and around the chicken.

To serve, season with flaky salt to taste. Not all of the butter needs to be eaten.

INDONESIAN CHICKEN SATE

SERVES 6

When you hear the words 'chicken sate', you might be thinking about that famously delicious chicken served at Thai restaurants with peanut sauce. That's a recipe I simply had to include in my book *The Curry Guy Thai*, because it's so popular. It's believed, however, that chicken sate originates from Indonesia, and this recipe is just like the chicken skewers I saw prepared there. The chicken is cooked on wooden skewers over a hot coconut-shell fire, basted heavily with kecap manis, which smokes heavily when it drips off and hits the coals, giving the chicken an amazing smoky flavour. This chicken sate is delicious served with the peanut sauce, lontong (see page 167), sambal oelek or another red hot sauce, and sliced cucumbers. You will need about 30 wooden skewers, soaked in water for 30 minutes.

PREP TIME: 15 MINS, PLUS MARINATING
COOKING TIME: 15 MINS

5 garlic cloves
2 tsp coriander seeds
1 tsp cumin seeds
2 tsp black peppercorns
3 tbsp kecap manis, plus extra as required
1 tbsp rapeseed (canola) oil
1kg (2lb 2oz) chicken thighs, cut into 2cm (¾in) pieces

FOR THE PEANUT SAUCE
Rapeseed (canola) oil, for frying
200g (2 cups) raw peanuts, skin on or off
4 small shallots, finely chopped
4 garlic cloves, roughly chopped
2.5cm (1in) piece of ginger
2 red spur chillies
2–3 red bird's eye chillies
70ml (¼ cup) kecap manis
2 tbsp light soy sauce
1 tsp palm sugar or light brown sugar (optional)
Salt, to taste if needed

Pound the garlic, coriander and cumin seeds and black peppercorns in a pestle and mortar until you have a paste. This can also be done in a spice grinder. Stir in the kecap manis and oil and then pour this marinade all over the chicken pieces in a large mixing bowl. Be sure to rub it right into the chicken pieces, cover and set aside to marinate for at least 30 minutes.

While the chicken is marinating, prepare the Indonesian-style peanut sauce. Pour about 10cm (4in) rapeseed (canola) oil into a saucepan or wok over a medium–high heat. When small bubbles begin to form, add the peanuts and fry until they turn a couple of shades darker – about 5 minutes should do. Transfer the fried peanuts to a bowl to cool. Discard (or save) all of the oil, except for about 2 tablespoons. Sauté the shallots, garlic, ginger and chillies for about 5 minutes to soften. Transfer these cooked ingredients to the bowl with the peanuts to cool a little. Using a pestle and mortar or food processor, grind to a coarse, not smooth, paste. Add the kecap manis and soy sauce and sugar, if needed, and stir to combine. Set aside.

When ready to cook, prepare your barbecue for direct heat cooking (see page 127). You want the coals to be white-hot! Your coals are ready when it is uncomfortably hot to hold your hand at cooking height for more than 2 seconds.

Skewer your chicken pieces on the wooden skewers. You only want about 4–5 pieces of chicken at the end of each skewer. Dip the marinated chicken in some more kecap manis until they are completely coated. I usually just pour about 250ml (1 cup) of kecap manis on a plate and roll the chicken in it. Place the skewers over the fire and cook for about 8 minutes, turning from time to time until the chicken is cooked through and nicely charred.

Season with salt to taste and serve hot with the peanut sauce.

KAGZHI KEBABS
SERVES 4

Who says the cheapest cuts of chicken can't be spectacular?! Yes, cooking with chicken drumsticks can be a bit fussy at times but these kagzhi kebabs are worth the effort! The meat you get from the chicken leg is some of the tastiest on the bird, not to mention that this is also great finger food, perfect for entertaining outdoors.

PREP TIME: 20 MINS
COOKING TIME: 55 MINS

12 chicken legs, skinned
Juice of 1 lemon
1 tbsp Kashmiri chilli powder, plus 2 tsp
2 tsp salt
4 tbsp garlic and ginger paste
2 tbsp ghee or rapeseed (canola) oil
1 medium red onion, finely chopped
2 tbsp flaked (slivered) almonds
2 tbsp pine nuts
125g (4½oz) paneer, grated or finely chopped
1 tsp garam masala (see page 161) or tandoori masala
3 tbsp double (heavy) cream
3 tbsp coriander (cilantro), finely chopped
Oil, for greasing

FOR BASTING
3 tbsp melted ghee
1 tbsp lemon juice
1 tbsp tikka masala powder

Pick up a chicken leg and locate the bone at the top. Carefully slice with a knife down the bone and use your finger to form a large pocket. Repeat with the remaining chicken legs.

Place the chicken legs in a large mixing bowl and add the lemon juice, 1 tablespoon of the chilli powder, the salt and 2 tablespoons of the garlic and ginger paste. Mix well to coat the chicken and set aside. Now melt the 2 tablespoons of ghee or oil in a frying pan (skillet) over a medium–high heat. When small bubbles begin to form, stir in the chopped red onion and fry for about 5 minutes or until soft and translucent. Add the remaining 2 tablespoons of garlic and ginger paste and fry for 30 seconds and then stir in the flaked (slivered) almond and pine nuts.

Stir it all together and then add the paneer, the remaining chilli powder and the garam or tandoori masala. Move it all around in the pan with your spatula until the cheese has softened and the spices are coating everything nicely – about 3 minutes should do the job. Take off the heat and stir in the double (heavy) cream. Allow to cool a little before stuffing it all into the pockets you prepared in the chicken legs.

To cook, prepare an indirect heat fire in your barbecue (see page 127), cover and bring to 220°C (425°F). This can also be done indoors in your oven at the same temperature. While your barbecue/oven is heating up, mix all the basting ingredients together and keep warm. Once your barbecue is up to heat, brush a little oil on the cooking grate on the cooler side of the cooking surface and place the chicken on the grate. If using an oven, place the chicken in a suitably sized roasting tray and place in the oven. Roast the chicken legs for about 45 minutes or until deliciously browned and cooked through. Baste with the melted ghee mixture a few times during cooking. Serve with green chilli and coriander chutney (see page 169) and chapattis, or whatever you think sounds good.

MALAI CHICKEN SEEKH KEBABS

SERVES 4–6

Cooking seekh kebabs on metal skewers over a hot fire takes practice. There is a real knack to squeezing the meat so tightly around the skewer that it doesn't all end up in the coals. Although that is my preferred method to cook seekh kebabs, this easier method works well too. Just lightly brush the cooking grate with a little oil and place the seekh kebab skewers right on the grate. Malai means 'cream' and that is an important ingredient in this recipe. It gives the kebabs amazing flavour and texture.

PREP TIME: 15 MINS
COOKING TIME: 20 MINS

6 garlic cloves
5cm (2in) piece of ginger
3 tbsp flaked (slivered) almonds
1–3 green bird's eye chillies
15g (¼ cup) mint leaves
15g (¼ cup) coriander (cilantro)
700g (1lb 9oz) minced
 (ground) chicken
1 tbsp melted beef or lamb
 fat (optional)
4 tbsp double (heavy) cream
1 tsp salt
1 tbsp lightly toasted coriander
 seeds, coarsely crushed
1 tsp ground cumin
2 tsp Kashmiri chilli powder
 (optional)
2 tbsp lemon juice
Oil, for greasing

FOR BASTING

3 tbsp melted ghee
1 tbsp lemon juice
1 tbsp tikka masala powder,
 garam masala (see page 161)
 or curry powder

Place the garlic, ginger, flaked (slivered) almonds, chillies, mint and coriander (cilantro) leaves on a cutting board and chop very finely. This can be done in a food processor but these ingredients should look very finely chopped and not like a paste. Pour these chopped ingredients into a large mixing bowl with the minced (ground) chicken and melted beef or lamb fat, if using. The fat is traditionally used to add more juiciness to the chicken. Work it all together with your hands like you're kneading dough to make bread. You really want to break the chicken down so that it is really smooth. This will give the kebabs that classic seekh kebab texture. If you're not in a rush, spend at least 5 minutes doing this.

Add the cream, salt, ground spices and lemon juice and mix it in using your hands until well combined. Cover and place in the fridge to marinate overnight or just carry on with the recipe. Marinating the chicken longer will produce tastier results though.

When ready to cook, prepare a direct heat fire on your barbecue (see page 127). Take a handful of the chicken mixture and roll it into a ball. Skewer it and squeeze it tightly around the skewer into a long sausage shape. Repeat with the remaining chicken. Then place the skewers on a lightly greased cooking grate and cook, turning regularly, until cooked through, which should only take about 10 minutes. While the chicken is cooking, whisk the basting ingredients together and use this ghee mixture to baste the chicken from time to time. Serve.

NOTE

Once you have the chicken combined with all the other ingredients, it is a good idea to take a small piece and fry it. This way you can try it and adjust the seasoning to taste before you skewer and cook the seekh kebabs over the fire.

GILAFI CHICKEN SEEKH KEBABS
SERVES 4

If you've tried my Chicken seekh kebabs from my blog or *The Curry Guy BBQ*, this recipe takes them to another level. It's essentially the same recipe but with a colourful exterior that will no doubt impress any guests you might be serving. The beef or lamb dripping that is mixed into the meat mixture is done a lot in India and Pakistan. It makes the chicken seekh kebabs, which have a tendency to be a bit dry, really juicy in the centre.

PREP TIME: 20 MINS
COOKING TIME: 15 MINS

½ red onion
3 garlic cloves, crushed
1.25cm (½in) piece of ginger, roughly chopped
3 green bird's eye chillies, roughly chopped
1 tbsp coriander (cilantro) (optional)
500g (1lb 2oz) minced (ground) chicken
2 tbsp beef or lamb dripping (homemade or shop-bought), melted
2 tsp ground cumin
2 tsp ground coriander
½ tsp garam masala (see page 161)
1 level tsp salt
1 tbsp Kashmiri chilli powder (more or less to taste)
Ghee, for basting

FOR THE EXTERIOR
½ red (bell) pepper
½ green (bell) pepper
½ yellow (bell) pepper
½ red onion

Grate or finely chop the onion and then place it on a porous cloth. Wrap it up tightly and squeeze out as much water as you can. You can discard the water. Now blend the onion, garlic, ginger, chillies and coriander (cilantro), if using, into a paste.

Place the minced (ground) chicken and the beef or lamb dripping in a food processor and blend until smooth. I usually do this in batches. Add the paste and the remaining ingredients, except the ghee. Place in the fridge to chill for at least 2 hours or overnight. Meanwhile, you can prepare the (bell) peppers and onion for the exterior. Finely chop them all and set aside. As you can see from the photo opposite, we're talking very finely chopped here.

When ready to cook, build a direct heat fire on your barbecue (see page 127). When it is uncomfortably hot to hold your hand 5cm (2in) above the cooking surface for longer than 2 seconds, your fire is ready. Wet your hands, take a ball of the chicken mixture and begin forming it around the skewer. Then mix all of the (bell) peppers and onion on a clean work surface and roll the chicken kebab in it. Sometimes it is easier to simply stick these chopped vegetables on the kebab. Be sure to keep your hands moist with water as you are doing this. This not only makes forming the kebabs easier, but it also gives them that smooth and authentic seekh kebab appearance and helps the chopped vegetables stick.

Lay your skewered seekh kebabs over the fire and be sure to rotate from time to time so that they cook evenly. When almost cooked through, baste with a little ghee. The cooking time varies depending on the size of your kebabs but it is usually about 10 minutes or until the internal heat reaches 75°C (165°F).

NOTE
If you are not experienced at squeezing minced chicken around metal skewers, you might find it easier to lightly grease the cooking grate and place the chicken seekh kebabs on top to cook. This will help prevent the meat falling off the skewers into the fire.

HONEY ROAST TANDOORI CHICKEN

SERVES 4

I really didn't want to give you another tandoori roast chicken like those in my other books. They are so good but there are other ways to prepare tandoori chicken, and this honey roast chicken is one of them.

PREP TIME: 30 MINS
COOKING TIME: 1 HOUR

1 x 1.5kg (3lb 5oz) whole chicken
Flaky salt and black pepper,
    to serve

FOR THE FIRST MARINADE
Juice of 2 large lemons
1 tbsp garlic and ginger paste
1 tsp salt
1 tbsp Kashmiri chilli powder
70ml (¼ cup) rapeseed
    (canola) oil

FOR THE SECOND MARINADE
5 tbsp ghee
2 medium red onions,
    finely chopped
3 green finger chillies
2 tsp ground cumin
1 tsp salt
1 tsp ground black pepper
½ tsp garam masala
    (see page 161)
100g (¼ cup) Greek yoghurt

TO FINISH
125ml (½ cup) honey

Using a sharp chef's knife or kitchen scissors, cut out the backbone of the chicken. Place the chicken breast-side up and crush it down with your hands. You should hear it crack as a few bones break.

Move your fingers under the skin of the chicken so that it is left on but not attached to the meat. Using a small, sharp knife, score the chicken meat all over the breasts, legs and thighs, being very careful not to rip the skin. Whisk the first marinade ingredients together in a bowl and then apply it to the chicken, inside, under the skin and on the skin too. Allow to marinate for 20 minutes or up to 2 hours while you prepare the second marinade.

Heat the ghee in a frying pan (skillet) and add the onions. Fry for about 10 minutes over a medium–high heat until the onions are golden brown and turning a bit crispy. Transfer them to a blender with a slotted spoon and pour any remaining ghee into a bowl with the honey, which will be used later. Set aside.

Add the chillies, ground cumin, salt, pepper and garam masala to the blender with the onions and blend to a paste. You can add a drop of water to do so if you must, but try not to. Pour this paste into a bowl and add the yoghurt. Whisk it all until creamy smooth.

Apply this marinade to the chicken inside, under the skin and over the skin, rubbing it right into the shallow scores you made in the meat. Allow to marinate for 4 hours or up to 24 hours. If time is an issue, you can go straight to cooking, but the longer you can marinate the chicken, the better.

Prepare your barbecue for indirect heat cooking (see page 127). You are aiming for a cooking temperature of 250°C (480°F). When your barbecue is up to heat, place the chicken breast-side up over the cooler side of the barbecue and close the lid. Allow to cook for 30 minutes. Transfer the chicken to a wire rack and allow to drip for a few minutes to dry and then apply the honey and ghee mixture all over the skin. Place the chicken back on the barbecue and continue roasting for another 20–30 minutes or until the internal temperature reaches 75°C (165°F). If you don't have a meat thermometer, the chicken is ready when the juices run clear when pricked with a knife or fork.

Season with flaky salt and more black pepper to serve.

VIETNAMESE-STYLE ROTISSERIE CHICKEN

SERVES 4

I love cooking rotisserie chicken but also understand that many people don't have rotisseries. So, if you do have one, try this recipe. If you don't, no problem! You can cook this chicken over indirect heat in the same way that the Honey roast tandoori chicken is cooked on page 141. You can cook it whole, as pictured, or butterfly the chicken as in the honey roast tandoori chicken recipe. Butterflying the chicken helps it cook faster when roasting. The flavour of this chicken is out of this world, so I really hope you give it a try, however you cook it. Please see the note about roasting in the oven or barbecue below.

PREP TIME: 30 MINS
COOKING TIME: 1½ HOURS

1 x 1.5kg (3lb 5oz) whole chicken
3 tbsp melted duck or goose fat
  (optional)
1–3 tsp freshly ground
  black pepper
Fresh red chillies, thinly sliced,
  to garnish

FOR THE MARINADE
2 lemongrass stalks, bruised and
  finely sliced
6 garlic cloves, finely chopped
2.5cm (1in) piece of ginger,
  finely chopped
6 coriander (cilantro) stalks,
  finely chopped
3 tbsp fish sauce
3 tbsp light soy sauce
2 tsp kecap manis

Mix all the marinade ingredients together in a mixing bowl. Then carefully slide your hand between the chicken skin and the meat. Apply the marinade under the skin and inside the cavity so that it gets right into the meat. If you have a little left over, you can also rub it over the skin. Allow to marinate while you set up your barbecue for indirect or rotisserie cooking, or leave it to marinate overnight. The longer the chicken marinates, the better.

Build a direct heat fire in your barbecue (see page 127). Once it's burning nicely, push the coals under where your rotisserie is. Secure the chicken on your rotisserie spit and rub it all over with the melted goose or duck fat, if using. This is optional but it does add a delicious flavour and helps make the skin crispy. Sprinkle the skin with the black pepper. I usually truss the chicken too to keep all that delicious flavour in and to help cook the chicken faster.

Place the chicken on the rotisserie on your barbecue. The rotisserie will now do all the work. This chicken should take 1½ hours to cook, and it's ready when a meat thermometer reads 74°C (165°F).

Once cooked, remove the chicken from your rotisserie and allow to rest for about 10 minutes before carving. This chicken is really good dipped into nước chấm (see page 163).

NOTE

If roasting the chicken in your barbecue, build a fire on one half of your barbecue. I use about one and a half chimney starters of charcoal, but how much you use will depend on your barbecue. Open both the bottom and top vents all the way and close the lid. You're aiming for a cooking temperature of 220°C (425°F). This temperature applies to cooking indoors in your oven too.

CHICKEN YAKITORI
SERVES 4

Not only does chicken yakitori taste amazing, it's also one of the easiest barbecue recipes I know. You don't even have to marinate the meat, as the marinade is brushed on it as it cooks. If you're looking for a light meal with very little fuss, this could well be exactly what you're looking for.

PREP TIME: 10 MINS
COOKING TIME: 30 MINS

1kg (2lb 2oz) boneless chicken
    thighs, skinned and cut into
    2.5 x 3.75cm (1 x 1½in) pieces
8 spring onions (scallions),
    white parts cut into 2.5cm
    (1in) pieces and green ends
    retained for the sauce
Oil, for greasing
2 tbsp sesame seeds, toasted
Dried chilli flakes (optional and
    to taste) *
Salt and pepper, to taste

**FOR THE YAKITORI SAUCE
(TARE)**
125ml (½ cup) light soy sauce
    or tamari
70ml (¼ cup) water
70ml (¼ cup) sake
125ml (½ cup) mirin rice wine
2 tsp ginger, finely chopped
    (minced)
2 garlic cloves, finely chopped
    (minced)
1 tbsp brown sugar
Green ends of spring onions
    (scallions), see above

Soak ten bamboo skewers in water for at least 30 minutes. While the skewers are soaking, place all the sauce ingredients in a saucepan and bring to a simmer over a high heat. Once simmering, reduce the heat to medium and simmer, uncovered, until the sauce has reduced by half.

Pour half the sauce into a serving bowl and allow to cool. Pour the remaining sauce into another bowl, which will be used for basting the chicken.

Skewer the chicken by folding each piece in half and then skewering them through both halves. Skewer two pieces of chicken followed by a piece of spring onion (scallion) and continue in this way until all the skewers are complete.

When ready to cook the chicken, build a medium direct heat fire on your barbecue (see page 127). You don't want the fire so hot that it chars the meat but, rather, browns it nicely. Be sure the cooking grate is really clean. When it is uncomfortable to hold your hand 5cm (2in) above the cooking surface for more than 2 seconds, your fire is ready. Season the cooking grate by rubbing it hard with a little oil. Do this and allow the oil to cook onto the grate and then repeat again. This will help stop the chicken from sticking to the grate.

Place the chicken skewers on the hot cooking grate and cook for about 4 minutes. Then turn to cook the other side. When the chicken skewers are about 70 per cent cooked through, either baste them generously with the yakitori sauce or dip them right into the sauce. Put back on the grill to cook through, turning and basting for a couple more minutes.

Sprinkle with the sesame seeds and chilli flakes, if using, then season with salt and pepper to taste. Serve hot with the reserved yakitori sauce.

*NOTE
Traditionally, ichimi tōgarashi, a fine Japanese chilli flake is used, but any will do.

INDONESIAN GRILLED CHICKEN
SERVES 6

There's grilled chicken and then there's grilled chicken the Indonesian way! Ayam bakar takes grilled chicken to a whole new and seriously amazing level. It really has to be one of the most delicious ways to cook chicken that I know of. The chicken is first braised in liquid that consists of aromatic ingredients and kecap manis and then allowed to sit in the hot liquid for 1 hour. Then it's thrown over hot coals. The result is sublime.

PREP TIME: 15 MINS
COOKING TIME: 1 HOUR
20 MINS

2 x 1.5kg (3lb 5oz) whole
   chickens
Juice of 1 lemon
4 tbsp coconut oil or rapeseed
   (canola) oil (I use coconut
   oil), plus extra for greasing
Salt and pepper, to taste

FOR THE PASTE
6 shallots
4 green bird's eye chillies
2 tbsp ground coriander
1 tbsp ground cumin
1 tsp ground turmeric
10 garlic cloves
5cm (2in) piece of ginger
2.5cm (1in) piece of galangal
4 makrut lime leaves, stalks
   removed and leaves
   roughly chopped

FOR THE BRAISING LIQUID
1 litre (4 cups) water
250ml (1 cup) kecap manis
1½ tbsp tamarind paste
3 lemongrass stalks, white part
   only, thinly sliced
5cm (2in) piece of galangal,
   sliced into thin pieces and
   lightly crushed
4 makrut lime leaves, left whole
1 tbsp palm sugar or light
   brown sugar

Place both chickens on a clean work surface, breast side up, and press down to flatten. You should hear some of the bones crack as you do this. Place the prepared chickens in a large mixing bowl and squeeze the lemon juice over them, rubbing the juice deep into the skin and flesh. Set aside.

Place all the paste ingredients in a food processor or blender and add just enough water to blend to a smooth paste. Now heat the oil in a large, high-sided pan or wok that has a lid. The pan needs to be large enough to cook both of the chickens. Add the prepared paste to the hot oil and fry for about 5 minutes, stirring regularly. You want to fry the paste until there is very little moisture and it looks a bit clumpy, but be careful not to brown the paste. Once you have a thick and fragrant paste, add all the braising liquid ingredients and bring to a simmer.

Place the chickens breast side down in the pan and ensure they are completely covered with the braising liquid by pushing them deep into it. Cover the pan and simmer for 15 minutes, then turn off the heat and allow the chickens to soak in the hot liquid for 1 hour. Do not remove the lid!

While the chickens are soaking, build a two-level direct heat fire (see page 127). Your fire is ready for cooking when it is uncomfortable for you to hold your hand 5cm (2in) above the grill for longer than 2 seconds. Spread the coals out so that there are more coals on one side of your barbecue, giving you an intense-heat cooking zone and a cooler area.

After the chickens have been soaking in the braising liquid for 1 hour, remove them to a platter and keep warm. Then turn the heat up on your stove and reduce the braising liquid until it is thick enough to coat the back of a wooden spoon. This will be used to baste the chickens on the barbecue. Season with a little salt and pepper to taste.

Now take your braised chickens out to the barbecue. Check the cooking heat again and lightly brush the cooking surface with oil. Place the chickens breast side up on the grill, slowly turning and basting with the braising liquid from time to time for about 20 minutes or until you have a nice char.

Allow to rest for about 5 minutes and serve.

CHICKEN LILIT
SERVES 4–6

You can cook Chicken lilit skewers indoors or out. While in Bali, we couldn't get enough of these and often ordered them from street-food stalls where the chicken lilit was cooked over hot coals. Personally, I think that is the best way to cook these skewers. The smoke adds a nice and subtle flavour. You can, however, cook these in a grill pan indoors in a little oil. Either way, I hope you give this recipe a try soon.

PREP TIME: 20 MINS
COOKING TIME: 10 MINS

3 tbsp rapeseed (canola) oil
700g (1lb 9oz) minced
    (ground) chicken
120g (1½ cups) fresh or frozen
    grated coconut
½ tsp salt
1 tsp sugar
10 lemongrass stalks
Oil, for greasing
Flaky salt, to taste
Hot sauce or kecap manis,
    for dipping

FOR THE SPICE PASTE

7 small shallots, roughly
    chopped
8 garlic cloves, smashed and
    roughly chopped
5cm (2in) piece of galangal,
    roughly chopped
½ tsp ground turmeric
2 cloves
2 red bird's eye chillies,
    roughly chopped
5 makrut lime leaves, stems
    removed and roughly chopped
4 candlenuts or macadamia nuts
3 tbsp lemongrass, white part
    only, finely chopped

Place all the spice paste ingredients in a food processor or pestle and mortar and grind to a fine paste. You can add a drop of water to assist grinding if needed.

Heat a frying pan (skillet) over a medium–high heat and add the oil. When visibly hot, stir in the blended spice paste and fry for about 3 minutes to cook out the rawness. Allow to cool completely.

Place the minced (ground) chicken in a mixing bowl and add the grated coconut, salt and sugar along with the cooled spice paste. Mix well with your hands so that everything is well combined. Place in the fridge until ready to cook. It's easiest to form the meat around the lemongrass skewers if it is cold.

When ready to get cooking, divide the chicken into ten equal-sized balls. Form these balls tightly around each piece of lemongrass into sausage shapes. It is easier to do this with wet hands.

To cook over fire, build a direct heat fire in your barbecue (see page 127). You want to use a good amount of charcoal so that it is searing hot. When it is uncomfortable to hold your hand 5cm (2in) above the cooking grate for longer than 2 seconds, your fire is ready. Lightly brush the cooking grate with a little oil and place the chicken on top. Cook for 5 minutes on one side and then carefully turn the skewers to cook the opposite side for another 5 minutes or until the chicken is cooked through.

To cook in a grill pan, heat a couple of tablespoons of oil in the pan over a medium–high heat. Place the skewers in the pan and cook for about 5 minutes per side or until the chicken is cooked through.

Serve hot, sprinkled with a bit of flaky salt to taste, with hot sauce or kecap manis to dip them in.

BASICS, ACCOMPANIMENTS AND SIDES

In this chapter you will find recipes for popular accompaniments and side dishes. These are what take your main dish and make it into a meal.

I think the most important part of this chapter, however, are the five Indian hotel (restaurant) gravies that I have wanted to share with you for some time. None of them are needed for the recipes in this book but you will learn how to make and use them, and yes, they can often be used to make these recipes as well as other Indian curries you might already know.

Although this is a chicken cookbook, I want to stress that these gravies can be used to whip up any curry quickly and easily. You can add the protein of your choice: chicken, lamb, beef... Or add paneer and/or veggies to make the curries vegetarian or vegan.

INDIAN HOTEL (RESTAURANT) BATCH GRAVIES

Look at any Indian curry recipe and you will notice that they all tend to start out in similar ways. A base masala is prepared and to that you add your protein or veggies of choice, water or stock, and voila...! You have yourself a curry.

The gravies you are going to learn here are staples in most upscale Indian hotel kitchens as well as many smaller but busy restaurants. When you make them, you can add them to a pan, stir in your protein and veggies and you've got an amazing curry in minutes.

Each of these gravies, with the exception of the white gravy, can be frozen and they are really convenient to have on hand. Using these five simple Indian hotel (restaurant) style base gravies, you are going to be able to get creative and make many more curries than a book this size could possibly feature.

If you have made my curry house-style curries using the UK-style base curry sauce from my other books, these base gravies take it all up a notch or two, especially when it comes to making more traditional Indian curries. In fact, hotel-style gravies were the inspiration behind the one-base-suits-all curry-house base sauce, as they help the chefs get hundreds of delicious curries to the table quickly and with minimum effort.

Hotel (restaurant) style curry gravies in India are incredible. They are slowly simmered and/or fried for optimum flavour and can be used immediately or stored in the fridge or freezer. Having been invited into the kitchens of quite a few upscale Indian restaurants in the UK, I know that these same gravies are used here too, as so many of the best chefs trained in Indian culinary schools. So if you've ever dined at a 5 star Indian restaurant and wondered how they produce so many amazing curries on such a large scale, this is how it's done!

Get ready to make the five most popular hotel-style gravies: tomato and onion, makhani, hariyali, white and onion.

HOW MANY DO THESE GRAVIES SERVE?

Generally speaking, 250ml (1 cup) of each gravy is enough for one restaurant-sized portion. So 1 litre (4 cups) will be enough to serve 4 people. If, one day, you are just cooking for yourself, you just need to use approximately 250ml (1 cup) of a gravy or a combination of two or three gravies.

The gravies will have already been slowly cooked to perfection so all you need to do is heat up some, then add some raw chicken or chicken tikka and you've got yourself a traditional Indian curry in minutes. If adding raw chicken, you will need to add a little water or stock to help cook it through. Do that and then simmer the sauce down to your desired consistency.

HOW TO USE THESE GRAVIES

Each of these five gravies is a curry in its own right. You could add chicken, lamb, beef, paneer or veggies to them and not be disappointed. They are, however, made in bulk and used as required. There is so much you can do with them. Try heating some makhani gravy in a pan and adding a little spinach hariyali and your makhani is transformed to a tomato-based saag. Mix the makhani gravy with some of the onion and tomato gravy and you'll have a butter chicken with onions. Butter chicken curry is made both with and without onions, so it is a thing.

Try making the tomato and onion gravy and adding a little white gravy and hariyali and, yet again, you'll have a delicious curry, and all you need to do is add chicken and/or some other main ingredients.

This is how these gravies are often used, a combination of two or three gravies, and the curries you can make using them will taste authentic, but they will also be your own 'chef's special' curries.

You really can't go wrong and, with a little experimentation, you could just come up with one of the best curries on the planet and it will be your own masterpiece! Give your curry the name you want, just like chefs do at so many restaurants.

Remember these are base gravies. So you might want to infuse a few chosen whole spices in some oil before adding them, just like you do in some of the other recipes in this book. Each of these hotel gravies taste great on their own or combined with the others.

TAILORING THESE GRAVIES TO TASTE

I have given you these gravy recipes as I saw them prepared. The cooking is in your hands though. If chillies or chilli powder are added to a gravy and you don't like spicy curries, add less or omit them completely, for example. Make these gravies the way you know you will like them.

In each of the following gravy recipes, I say to add salt to taste at the end of the recipe. You could just leave the salt out if you are going to be using the gravies in future. You can always add salt to taste to the finished curry you are making.

UPSCALING AND DOWNSCALING

Hotel-style gravies are made in large batches at restaurants so that the chefs have them prepared and at the ready when needed. My recipes will make enough gravy for at least 2 curries that serve 4 or more if used in combination with the other hotel gravies. These will keep in the fridge for up to 3 days, and all of them, except for the white gravy, will freeze well. If you're planning a big curry feast, you can upscale them accordingly by doubling or tripling the recipes. Just be careful not to double spicy ingredients like chilli powder or chillies. Add these to taste. If you are making a large batch and intend to freeze it, be sure to freeze in portions that will be convenient for use.

Each of the following recipes are listed in order of importance, and the amount each recipe makes correlates with this. For example, you will probably use the tomato and onion gravy first much more than the onion or white gravies, though both of the latter can actually easily be made into a finished curry.

TOMATO AND ONION GRAVY

MAKES 2 LITRES (8 CUPS)

So many curries start with a base masala of onions and tomatoes. Indian curries like South Indian chicken drumstick curry (page 63), Chicken changezi (page 71) and Punjabi ginger chicken curry (page 81) to name just a few but there are countless examples. Of course, each of those examples have their own unique spice blends and you can use this tomato and onion gravy and still adjust the flavours accordingly by looking at and following the recipes. At busy restaurants where the chefs have no idea what exactly is going to be ordered, it's batches of tomato and onion gravy that really make things easier. Check out pages 152–3 to better understand how you can use this gravy on its own or in combination with one or two of the other gravies.

PREP TIME: 20 MINS
COOKING TIME: 40 MINS

70ml (¼ cup) rapeseed
    (canola) oil
3 green cardamom pods,
    smashed
2 cloves
5cm (2in) cinnamon stick
2 Indian bay leaves (cassia
    leaves)
1kg (2lb 2oz) onions,
    roughly chopped
1 tsp salt
4 tbsp garlic and ginger paste
3 green chillies, roughly
    chopped
2 tbsp ground cumin
2 tbsp ground coriander
2 tbsp Kashmiri chilli powder
    (more or less to taste)
1 tsp ground turmeric
About 70ml (¼ cup) water
1kg (2lb 2oz) chopped tomatoes,
    tinned (canned) are fine
5 tbsp coriander (cilantro),
    roughly chopped
2 tsp kasoori methi (dried
    fenugreek leaves)

Heat the oil in a large saucepan over a medium heat. When bubbles begin to form, stir in the whole spices and bay leaves and let them infuse their flavour into the oil. Stir in the chopped onions and salt and fry for about 15 minutes or until the onions are soft and turning a deep golden brown in colour. The salt will help release moisture from the onions and cook them faster.

Stir in the garlic and ginger paste and then the chopped chillies. Then add the ground cumin, coriander, chilli powder and turmeric. Stir the spices into the onion mixture along with the water so that the spices don't burn. Add the chopped tomatoes and bring it all to a simmer. Cover the pan and simmer for about 10 minutes. When you lift the lid, the oil will have separated and floated to the top. Stir this back in and add the chopped coriander (cilantro) and the kasoori methi (dried fenugreek leaves) by rubbing them between your fingers. Take the pan off the heat and allow to cool. If you prefer a smoother sauce, blend it until smooth or just leave it as it is.

Season with more salt, if needed to taste. Then use immediately, store the gravy in the fridge for up to 3 days or freeze it in 250ml (1 cup) portions for up to 6 months.

MAKHANI GRAVY
MAKES ABOUT 1.25 LITRES (5 CUPS) BEFORE THE CREAM AND BUTTER

If you've ever tried an authentic Butter chicken in New Delhi, this sauce or one like it will most definitely be used. This is a smooth tomato gravy that only becomes a 'makhani' gravy when the butter and cream are added. 'Makhani' means 'butter' in Hindi. I don't add the butter or cream when making this, as cream doesn't freeze well. Without the butter and cream, this gravy can also be added to any bold curry when a delicious tomato flavour is desired. If you do add the butter and cream, you'll have a butter chicken sauce that can be added to tandoori chicken, along with any excess marinade to make the most amazing hotel-style butter chicken. For a better understanding about how this gravy can be used, please see pages 152–3.

PREP TIME: 10 MINS
COOKING TIME: 40 MINS

4 tbsp rapeseed (canola) oil
3 green cardamom pods,
    seeds only
6 black peppercorns
5cm (2in) cinnamon stick
3 tbsp garlic ginger paste
2 tbsp Kashmiri chilli powder
    (or paprika for a milder
    flavour)
1.2kg (2lb 10oz) chopped tinned
    (canned) tomatoes or
    unseasoned passata
2 green finger chillies, cut
    lengthwise (optional for
    more heat)
100g (¾ cup) cashews
Salt, to taste

OPTIONAL INGREDIENTS
125ml (½ cup) single (light)
    cream (more or less to taste)
4 tbsp butter

Heat the oil in a large saucepan over a medium–high heat. When small bubbles begin to form, stir in the cardamom seeds, black peppercorns and cinnamon stick and infuse these flavours into the oil for about 30 seconds. Stir in the garlic and ginger paste and let it sizzle for about 30 seconds and then add the chilli powder or paprika and stir it into the oil. Add the chopped tomatoes or passata and sliced chillies, if using.

Bring to a simmer. While the sauce is heating up, blend the cashews with just enough water to make a smooth paste and stir it in. Cover the pan and simmer over a medium heat for about 30 minutes. If you would like to, you could blend this sauce to break down the whole spices and chillies but I rarely do that. You could just fish out the chillies and cinnamon stick too. Season with salt to taste.

To make this a makhani sauce, stir in the cream and butter. If you are freezing this sauce, I recommend not doing that though, as it is better to add the cream and butter fresh when you are making your next butter chicken or another curry.

NOTE

This sauce has so many possible uses. You could add it to any curry that needs a bit more tomato flavour in small or large amounts to taste. You could also add it to paneer for a butter paneer or use it instead of tomato purée (paste) or passata when called for in an Indian recipe. Just get creative and have fun experimenting.

HARIYALI (GREEN) GRAVY
MAKES ABOUT 1 LITRE (4 CUPS)

This hariyali gravy is added to curries to give them a green tone with the flavours of spinach, mint and coriander (cilantro). Let's say, for example, you have made the Chicken shahi korma (page 66) and you just want to change it some. You could give it a different colour and change the flavour profile by stirring in some of this tasty green gravy. It is, of course, a good curry in its own right but can also be very colourful and delicious added to other curries to taste.

PREP TIME: 10 MINS
COOKING TIME: 20 MINS

500g (1lb 2oz) baby spinach leaves, washed and roughly chopped
2–3 tbsp rapeseed (canola) oil
2 medium onions, finely chopped
2 tbsp garlic and ginger paste
6 green finger chillies, roughly chopped
160g (5¾oz) mint leaves, washed and roughly chopped
400g (14oz) coriander (cilantro), roughly chopped

Bring a pan of water to the boil and add the spinach. Blanch the spinach for about a minute and then strain. If you place the blanched spinach in a bowl of iced water, it will help retain the bright green colour, but that is done more for presentation than flavour.

Now heat the oil in a frying pan (skillet) over a medium–high heat and fry the chopped onions for about 5 minutes or until soft and translucent. Add the garlic and ginger paste and the chopped chillies and fry for a further minute. Stir in the mint and coriander (cilantro) and reduce the heat to low. Stir for a couple of minutes until the greens have wilted some into the oil but still look fresh.

Place this mixture in a bowl and add the blanched spinach. Allow it all to cool completely and then blend it to a smooth paste. That's it. Your smooth hariyali gravy is ready to add to any curry you like and will keep, covered tightly, in the fridge for up to 3 days, or you could freeze it for up to 2 months with little loss of flavour and colour.

WHITE GRAVY
MAKES 1 LITRE (4 CUPS)

This white gravy can be used to quickly make a curry that is nutty and creamy, such as the White chicken shahi kofta korma on page 68. It can also be used to just give a curry a bit of nutty and creamy flavour or cool down a curry that is too spicy, even when the recipe doesn't call for it. Leave the chillies out of this gravy and you will have something very similar to the sauce used in a curry house-style chicken korma. Curry-house kormas are usually quite sweet, so you could heat up some of this, then add your chicken and sugar to taste. This gravy does not freeze well, so you might want to halve the recipe.

PREP TIME: 15 MINS
COOKING TIME: 15 MINS

3 tbsp rapeseed (canola) oil, plus 2 tbsp
500g (1lb 2oz) onions, roughly chopped
110g (3¾oz) melon seeds
110g (3¾oz) cashews
1 tbsp garlic and ginger paste
70ml (¼ cup) single (light) cream
125ml (1 cup) plain natural yoghurt
2 green cardamom pods, lightly bruised
2.5cm (1in) cinnamon stick
3 green finger chillies, slit lengthwise down the centre (optional)
Salt and freshly ground black pepper, to taste

Heat the 3 tablespoons of oil in a large saucepan over a medium heat. When hot, add the chopped onions and fry for about 5 minutes to soften. Then stir in the melon seeds and cashews and continue frying over a medium heat to cook everything through. You don't want to brown the cashews and seeds but rather cook out the rawness for a few more minutes, so stir often. Stir in the garlic and ginger paste and fry for another 30 seconds. Turn off the heat and allow to cool.

Now transfer it all to a blender and add the cream and yoghurt. Blend to a smooth paste and set aside. In the same pan, heat the 2 tablespoons of oil over a medium–high heat. Stir in the whole spices and let them infuse their flavour into the oil. Then pour in the blended paste. You don't want to lose a drop, so add a little water to your blender, swish it around and pour it all in. Add the green chillies, if using, and bring to a simmer and add ground pepper and salt to taste.

You can store this gravy in the fridge for up to 3 days.

NOTE
If you prefer a spicy curry, the green chillies can be added with the cream and yoghurt and blended with the other ingredients.

ONION GRAVY

MAKES 750ML (3 CUPS)

Onion gravy is delicious stirred into any bold curry such as a changezi (page 71), madras or dopiaza. With this onion gravy recipe, however, I want to give you a quick curry recipe that I literally made up one day. After the gravy was finished cooking, I froze half and left the rest in the pan. I then stirred in a handful of chopped coriander (cilantro) and 3 large handfuls of fresh methi (fenugreek) leaves. Then I added about 700g (1lb 9oz) of chicken that I had marinated in a simple yoghurt, salt and lemon marinade. I added the chicken and all the marinade, covered the pan and simmered until the chicken was cooked through, and we all enjoyed an amazing chicken methi curry. If I had had any on hand at the time, I would have stirred in a little white gravy too. That's how each of these hotel gravy recipes can be used. If it sounds good to add something, it probably will be.

PREP TIME: 15 MINS
COOKING TIME: 25 MINS

70ml (¼ cup) rapeseed
    (canola) oil
2 star anise
6 green cardamom pods,
    lightly bruised
5cm (2in) cinnamon stick
1 tsp black peppercorns
2 Indian bay leaves
    (cassia leaves)
1kg (2lb 2oz) onions,
    finely chopped
2 tbsp garlic and ginger paste
1 tbsp ground cumin
2 tbsp ground coriander
1 tsp ground turmeric
2 tbsp Kashmiri chilli powder
    (more or less to taste)
125ml (½ cup) water
Salt, to taste

Heat the oil in a large saucepan over a medium–high heat. Add the whole spices and Indian bay leaves and let them infuse into the hot oil for about 30 seconds. Stir in the chopped onions and fry for 10–15 minutes or until they are a deep, rather dark, golden brown. Add the garlic and ginger paste and the ground spices and stir them in. Then add the water, which is done so that the spices don't burn and become bitter.

At this stage, you could allow the onion gravy to cool and blend it until smooth. That's up to you, but I usually leave it as is. Reduce the heat to low and cover the gravy or blended gravy to simmer gently for about 5 minutes. You can add a little more water if it is looking dry. Season with salt to taste.

This gravy can be stored in the fridge for up to 3 days. You can also portion it out into convenient-sized containers for up to 6 months.

CHICKEN STOCK
MAKES 3½ LITRES (14 CUPS)

First of all, I would like to stress that using homemade chicken stock when stock is called for in a recipe will get you better results. Good stocks are the backbone of many recipes. I rarely add salt to my stocks as I prefer to do this at the cooking stage of whatever I plan to prepare. You can easily upscale or downscale this recipe. This is a good multi-purpose stock. You can tweak the recipe depending on what it is you're cooking. For example, adding a little galangal and lemongrass will be perfect for most Southeast Asian dishes.

PREP TIME: 15 MINS
COOKING TIME: 4 HOURS

1.5kg (3lb 5oz) chicken bones
1 x 2.5kg (5lb) whole chicken
6 litres (24 cups) cold water

AROMATIC INGREDIENTS
5cm (2in) piece of ginger, thinly
   sliced and lightly crushed
8 garlic cloves, smashed
8 spring onions (scallions)
1 onion, peeled and quartered
2 carrots, roughly chopped
½ bunch of coriander (cilantro)
20 black peppercorns

Place the chicken bones and chicken in a 6-litre (6-quart) pot and cover with the water. Bring to the boil and simmer for 5 minutes. Then strain the stock and discard the liquid. This step is optional but it will result in a clearer stock.

Wash the stock pot and put the bones and chicken back in it. Add the aromatic ingredients. Cover with 5 litres (4½ quarts) of water and bring to the boil over a medium heat. Once boiling, reduce the heat to medium and slowly simmer for 4 hours, skimming off any foam that rises to the top.

Once the stock has been simmering for 4 hours, strain the stock into a bowl. Discard the bones and aromatic ingredients. The whole chicken will be overcooked but the meat is great in sandwiches or stirred into a soup or sauce, so don't throw that away.

Allow the stock to cool a little and then place it, covered, in the fridge for up to 3 days. This stock can be frozen for up to 6 months. Just defrost it and use the stock in recipes that call for unsalted chicken stock. Be sure to freeze the stock in portion sizes that are convenient for you. I usually freeze it in 500ml (2-cup) portions which are convenient for soups and then freeze some in ice-cube trays for when I just need a little stock. If freezing in ice-cube trays, you can empty them into a freezer bag and always have homemade stock cubes on hand whenever you need them.

NOTE

If you happen to have a countertop pressure cooker and/or slow cooker, you can use them for this recipe. If using a pressure cooker, set it to high with all the ingredients in the pot and pressure-cook for about 4 minutes before allowing it to naturally release the pressure. If using a slow cooker, add all the ingredients and set it to stew for 8–12 hours, the longer, the better. I have let mine stew for up to 24 hours with great results.

GARAM MASALA

MAKES ABOUT 10 TABLESPOONS (110G/1 CUP)

There are countless recipes for garam masala. Garam means 'warming' and masala means 'mixture'. So garam masala is a mixture of warming spices. The spices used can vary depending on what is being made, but this all-purpose blend will get you much better results than what you will get from your local supermarket. I tend to double or triple this recipe so that I always have some on hand. Garam masala is best prepared on the day you are serving it, however, so if I am preparing a special dinner, I'll make a small amount to use in the recipe.

PREP TIME: 10 MINS
COOKING TIME: 5 MINS

3 heaping tbsp coriander seeds
3 heaping tbsp cumin seeds
3 tsp black peppercorns
2 heaping tbsp fennel seeds
1½ tsp cloves
5cm (2in) cinnamon stick
2 dried Indian bay leaves (cassia leaves, optional)
10 green cardamom pods, seeds only
1 blade mace

Toast all the spices in a dry frying pan (skillet) over a medium–high heat until fragrant and warm to the touch but not yet smoking, moving them around in the pan and being careful not to burn them. If they begin to smoke, take them off the heat. Tip the warm spices onto a plate and leave to cool.

When cool, grind the spices to a fine powder in a spice grinder or with a pestle and mortar. Store in an airtight container in a cool, dark place and use within 2 months for optimal flavour.

GARLIC AND GINGER (AND CHILLI) PASTE

MAKES 15 GENEROUS TABLESPOONS

Many of the recipes in this book call for garlic and ginger paste. Some call for garlic, ginger and chilli paste. The method for making both is the same and the amount you blend is completely down to your requirements. To give you an idea how much to make, I have given an exact recipe for my garlic and ginger paste below which makes 15 generous tablespoons or enough garlic and ginger paste for about seven curries. To make garlic, ginger and chilli paste, just add chillies to the blend to taste.

PREP TIME: 5 MINS

150g (5½oz) garlic, roughly chopped
150g (5½oz) ginger, roughly chopped
Green bird's eye chillies, to taste (optional)

For garlic and ginger paste, simply blend equal amounts of peeled garlic cloves and ginger with a drop of water in a blender or spice grinder to make a paste.

To make garlic, ginger and chilli paste, blend the garlic and ginger as above, then add the chillies to taste and blend again; start with a small amount and then taste and add more as required.

This will keep, covered, in the fridge for 3 days but can also be frozen; freeze in ice-cube trays to give you handy tablespoon-sized portions.

CHICKEN FLOSS

MAKES 225G (3¼ CUPS)

Chicken floss is loved all over China and Southeast Asia. This recipe can also be prepared with other meats but, as this is a chicken cookbook, we're sticking to chicken here. In Southeast Asia, chicken floss can be found in large containers in shops, ready prepared. It is also a popular sandwich filling. Try adding a large amount to the Bánh mì on page 115 and you won't be disappointed. It is pictured next to the bánh mì in that recipe. This recipe can easily be scaled up and, as it takes so long to make, you might want to consider doing that.

PREP TIME: 30 MINS
COOKING TIME: 2 HOURS

750g (1lb 10oz/approx. 2 large)
    chicken breasts, skinned
1 litre (4 cups) water
4 spring onions (scallions),
    left whole
2 lemongrass stalks, smashed
2.5cm (1in) piece of ginger,
    thinly sliced
8 dried bird's eye chillies
    or similar
3 tbsp Chinese rice wine or
    dry sherry
4 tbsp light soy sauce
2 tbsp fish sauce

TO FINISH
1 tbsp rapeseed (canola) oil
1 tsp sugar
½ tsp chilli powder or to taste
½ tsp ground white pepper
1 tbsp light soy sauce

First, you need to cut the chicken and it is very important how you do this! You want to cut the chicken breasts into 1.25cm (½in) slices with the grain of the meat. When you look at a slice, you should see long grains going through each slice. You will be tearing this chicken into floss, so you should be able to visualize how this would be done.

Place the sliced chicken in a saucepan and add the water and everything up to and including the fish sauce. Bring to the boil over a high heat and then reduce the heat to low and simmer for about 45 minutes. Skim off any foam that rises to the top. After 45 minutes of simmering over a low heat, transfer the chicken pieces to a plate to cool.

Once cooled, shred the chicken into floss-like pieces using your hands or a couple of forks. The finer you can shred the chicken, the better. This is going to take some time, especially if you upscaled the recipe.

With the chicken shredded, place a large frying pan (skillet) over a low heat and stir in the oil, sugar, chilli powder and white pepper. Add the shredded chicken and soy sauce and stir well to combine. It will look quite dry but this is chicken floss after all. Continue cooking over this low heat for about 45 minutes, stirring and pulling the chicken apart more as you do until it is dried and looks fluffy and flossy. This meat is now cured, just like beef jerky is dried and cured, so it should keep for a very long time in an airtight container in a cool, dark place like a cupboard. I usually freeze it though in small portions to ensure it remains fresh.

NƯỚC CHẤM

SERVES 4

This Vietnamese dipping sauce also makes a delicious marinade. You will need to taste as you go to achieve the best flavour combination. This sauce is so good with the Vietnamese whole boiled chicken on page 82.

PREP TIME: 5 MINS

70ml (¼ cup) fish sauce
125ml (½ cup) water
3 tbsp sugar (approx. and to taste)
1 tbsp distilled white vinegar
3 tbsp lime juice
2 garlic cloves, finely chopped
2 red finger chillies, finely chopped (more or less to taste)
2 tbsp finely chopped carrot
5cm (2in) lemongrass, white part only, very thinly sliced (optional)

Place all of the ingredients up to and including the chillies in a mixing bowl and whisk until the sugar has dissolved. It keeps in the fridge for up to 3 days. Add the carrot and lemongrass, if using, just before serving so it stays crunchy.

THAI CUCUMBER SALAD

SERVES 2–4

This easy salad is great as a side for many curries. Not just Thai! Though it is in my opinion a must with the Thai chicken biryani on page 92.

PREP TIME: 5 MINS
COOKING TIME: 5 MINS

8 tbsp water
8 tbsp sugar
8 tbsp white vinegar
1 English cucumber, seeded and roughly chopped
2–3 shallots, roughly chopped
6 green finger chillies, sliced into thin rings
4 red spur chillies, roughly chopped
Salt, to taste

Pour the water, sugar and white vinegar into a small saucepan and bring to a simmer. The sugar will dissolve into the liquid. Continue simmering until reduced by about half and slightly syrupy. Place in the fridge to cool. Once cooled, add the chopped cucumber, shallots and chillies and season with a little salt to taste. Keep covered in the fridge until ready to serve.

STEAMED WHITE BASMATI RICE
SERVES 4

This is my no-fail fluffy basmati rice recipe. You will make perfect rice every time with this recipe. Of course, most rice packets come with cooking instructions, so feel free to use those too, but I think you're going to love the results you get here.

PREP TIME: 2 MINS,
PLUS SOAKING
COOKING TIME: 40 MINS

370g (2 cups) basmati rice
750ml (3¼ cups) cold water
Pinch of salt
1 tbsp ghee or butter

Put the uncooked rice in a large bowl and cover with cold water from the tap. Swirl the water around with your hands; it will become milky from the rice starch. Pour the water out, add fresh water and repeat until the water is almost clear. About five times should do the job. Leave the rice to soak in the last batch of fresh water for about 30 minutes, then drain.

Place the rice in a saucepan along with the measured cold water, salt and ghee or butter. Cover with a tight-fitting lid and bring to the boil over a high heat. As soon as the water boils, remove from the heat and let it sit, lid on, for 40 minutes. Don't remove the lid. After 40 minutes, your rice will be perfectly done. Using a fork or chopstick, separate the rice grains, stirring very slowly. Basmati rice has a tendency to turn to mush if stirred too vigorously.

INSTANT PARATHAS
MAKES 4

Parathas are a bit fussy to make, and as there are only a couple of recipes in the book that call for them, I decided to give you my paratha hack, which works perfectly. You could also purchase parathas in the frozen section of Indian grocers, which are really good. This recipe makes four parathas but you can easily scale it up to make as many as you like. Using a non-stick pan is essential for success. A non-stick tawa is even better.

PREP TIME: 20 MINS
COOKING TIME: 10 MINS

250g (2 cups) plain (all-purpose) flour
1 tsp salt
250ml (1 cup) water
1 tbsp rapeseed (canola) oil
4 tbsp ghee or rapeseed (canola) oil

Sift the flour into a mixing bowl and then whisk in the salt, water and the tablespoon of rapeseed (canola) oil. This will make a batter that is very similar in consistency to American pancakes. Place a non-stick frying pan (skillet) over a high heat. Add 1 tablespoon of the ghee or oil to the pan and swirl it around to coat.

Pour a ladleful of the batter into the centre of the pan and then spread it out in a circular motion with the bottom of the ladle. Fry for 1–2 minutes, or until lightly toasted on the bottom, then flip it over to cook the other side. Keep the cooked parathas warm while you cook the rest.

NAANS
MAKES 6

I have featured quite a few different naan recipes in my previous books. This is the recipe I use most often. The recipe makes either pillowy fluffy naans or crispy naans, depending on how thinly you roll the dough.

PREP TIME: 20 MINS,
PLUS RISING
COOKING TIME: 20 MINS

500g (4 cups) plain (all-purpose) flour, plus extra for dusting
½ tbsp salt
1 tbsp baking powder
150ml (⅔ cup) full-fat (whole) milk
7g (2½ tsp) fast-action dried yeast
2 tbsp sugar
2 eggs
135g (generous ½ cup) Greek yoghurt
Oil, for greasing (optional)
3 tbsp melted ghee
Nigella seeds (black onion seeds) and/or sesame seeds, for sprinkling

Sift the flour, salt and baking powder into a large bowl. Warm the milk in the microwave or in a small pan on the hob until hand-hot. Pour into a jug, add the yeast and sugar and whisk together. Cover with a cloth and leave in a warm place for about 20 minutes. It should foam up. If it doesn't, don't worry, your naans will still rise.

Lightly beat the eggs and yoghurt together. Pour the yeasty milk mixture into the flour, along with the whisked eggs and yoghurt, and mix everything to combine.

Tip the dough out onto a clean work surface and knead for about 10 minutes until you have a soft, slightly sticky ball of dough. Brush the insides of the bowl with a little oil and place the dough back in the bowl. Cover and leave to rise for 1 hour, or up to 24 hours – longer rising times achieve a better flavour.

Once risen, pull off a tennis-ball-sized chunk of dough and, using your hands or a rolling pin, roll it out on a lightly floured work surface into a flat, circular disc or teardrop shape, about 5mm (¼in) thick. Slap the disc between your hands to remove the excess flour.

Heat a dry frying pan (skillet) over a high heat and, when very hot, place the naan in it. It will begin to cook on the underside, then bubble on the top. Check the bottom regularly to ensure it doesn't burn. If it begins to get too dark, turn the naan over to get a bit of colour on the other side. Each naan should take no more than 3–5 minutes to cook. This can also be done on a lightly greased barbecue grill with no pan.

Transfer the cooked naan to a plate, brush with a little ghee and sprinkle with nigella and/or sesame seeds. Keep warm while you cook the remaining dough in the same way.

NOTE

If you are cooking on a gas burner and have a pan that is not non-stick, such as cast iron, you can get fantastic results with this recipe. Lightly dampen the rolled naan dough with water and slap it hard, wet side down, into the pan so that it sticks to the pan. Allow bubbles to form on the top and then turn your pan towards the gas flame to brown the bubbles, which will become even larger as you do. Then remove the naan with a metal spatula.

RUMALI ROTIS

SERVES 4–8

Rumali rotis are paper thin rotis. They're lighter than most and are the perfect accompaniment for the Grilled butter chicken (page 130) and the Chicken shami kebabs (page 111). They also make great wraps.

**PREP TIME: 20 MINS,
PLUS RISING
COOKING TIME: 10 MINS**

250g (2 cups) plain (all-purpose)
   flour, plus extra for dusting
1 tsp table salt
1 tsp sugar
2 tbsp rapeseed (canola) oil
250ml (1 cup) hand-hot milk

FOR COOKING
3 tbsp salt
250ml (1 cup) water

Sift the flour into a large mixing bowl. Add the 1 teaspoon of salt, the sugar and the oil, then slowly pour in the warm milk, working it in with your hand. Form into a soft dough and knead for at least 10 minutes on a flour-dusted surface. You do not want to add too much flour – just enough so that the dough is not sticking to your hands but is still soft. Form this into a smooth dough ball by kneading it for about 5 minutes, then cover with a damp cloth. Allow to rest for at least 2 hours and up to 6 hours.

When ready to cook, separate the dough into eight small balls or four large balls. I like them large for wrapping, but the smaller balls may be better for light snacks. Using a rolling pin, roll out one of the balls into a circle. You want the rotis to be as thin as you can get them. Paper thin! I usually roll out and cook the rotis one at a time for ease.

Stir the 3 tablespoons of salt into the water until all of the salt has dissolved. Now heat a pan that is not non-stick over a high heat. You want your pan to be flaming hot before adding your first roti. Dip your hand in the salt water mixture and splash it all over the surface of the pan. Do this a few times so that the whole surface is covered. The pan surface will turn white from the salt, which adds flavour and also stops the rumali rotis from sticking to the pan.

Place your first roti in the pan and cook for about 15 seconds. Carefully flip it over and you will see light brown spots, which is good. Allow to cook on this side for 3 seconds, then flip again for 3 seconds and once again for 3 seconds.

Remove the rumali roti from the pan and fold it into a square shape. Cover to keep warm. Repeat with the remaining dough, splashing a little more salt water into the pan. This will cool it down some and also ensure your remaining rotis don't stick.

Repeat the folding process for each roti and cover to keep warm. These are best served immediately while they are still hot from the pan but you can keep them, covered, for about 30 minutes if needed.

NOTE

If you are making really large rumali rotis, you can do this with an upturned wok. Heat the wok over a high heat and, when flaming hot, turn it over. Splash the top with the salt and water mixture and then drape your roti over the top. Just keep flipping as in the above pan method until cooked through.

INDONESIAN RICE CAKES

SERVES 4–6

These delicious rice cakes, lontong, are the perfect accompaniment for Indonesian chicken sate (page 133) where you will see sliced lontong photographed. They are also good stirred into any Southeast Asian curry. When adding them to a curry, they can be used as a unique and tasty substitute for serving the curry over rice.

PREP TIME: 10 MINS
COOKING TIME: 40 MINS

450g (1½ cups) jasmine rice
650ml (2¾ cups) water
Approx. 4 banana leaves, washed
    with warm water

Place the rice in a bowl and wash with several changes of water. At first, the starch from the rice will make the water milky. With each change of water, the water will become clearer. Once the water is almost clear, the rice is ready for cooking.

Place the rinsed rice in a saucepan and add the measured water until there is enough to cover the rice by 2.5cm (1in). Bring the water to the boil over a high heat and then reduce the heat to low and cover the pan with a tight-fitting lid. Simmer over a low heat for 20 minutes. Turn off the heat and transfer the rice to a plate to cool a little.

Meanwhile, cut the banana leaves into roughly 30cm (12in) squares. Wet your hands, take a large handful of the rice and form it into a cylinder shape that is about 26cm (8in) long and neatly flattened on each end. Put a banana leaf square in front of you and place the cylinder of rice at the bottom, nearest you. There should be at least 5cm (2in) of banana leaf on each side of the rice. Roll it all up around the rice and secure the ends by tying them or skewering them with a toothpick. Repeat with the remaining rice.

Now place all the banana leaf rice rolls in a large pot and cover with water. The rolled rice needs to be completely submerged in water. Bring to the boil and then simmer for about 20 minutes. The rice cakes are ready when the rice expands in the banana leaves. They will look tightly packed. Remove from the water and allow to cool completely, then carefully remove the banana leaves. Using a wet knife, slice into bite-sized circles. These will keep in the fridge for 3 days or can be used/eaten immediately.

ALL-PURPOSE TANDOORI MARINADE

MAKES 300ML (1¼ CUPS)

This is a simple marinade that works well with chicken and other meats, as well as veggies and paneer. Before adding this marinade, rub your meat of choice with the juice of 1 lemon, a little salt and some garlic and ginger paste for added flavour. Let this first marinade soak into the meat and then add the tandoori marinade. You can marinate the meat in this marinade for as little as 30 minutes or up to 2 days. The longer, the better.

PREP TIME: 10 MINS

250ml (1 cup) Greek yoghurt
1 tbsp rapeseed (canola) oil
2 tbsp garlic and ginger paste
3 green finger chillies, roughly chopped
1 small bunch of coriander (cilantro), roughly chopped
2 tsp ground coriander
2 tsp tandoori masala
2 tsp ground cumin
1 tbsp Kashmiri chilli powder
1 tbsp smoked paprika or more chilli powder
Juice of 2 limes
1 tsp salt

Place all the ingredients in a blender or food processor and blend to a smooth paste. Try it and adjust the ingredients to taste. Place in the fridge until ready to use. You can marinate chicken in this marinade for up to 2 days. Just before cooking the meat, rub off as much marinade as possible. The marinade can also be stirred in small amounts into curries for added flavour.

MINT RAITA

MAKES 250ML (1 CUP)

You will probably recognize the flavour of this raita as it is popular at curry houses all over the world. Sometimes it is dyed green but I rarely do this. This is a quick and easy raita that goes well with tandoori chicken, samosas and frankies (see pages 26, 21 and 121).

PREP TIME: 10 MINS
COOKING TIME: 3 MINS

1 tsp cumin seeds
2 tbsp coriander (cilantro)
1 garlic clove
1 green finger chilli
250ml (1 cup) Greek yoghurt
3 tbsp smooth mango chutney
1 tbsp mint sauce
1–2 tbsp milk (optional)
1–2 tsp sugar, or to taste
Salt, to taste

Heat a small frying pan (skillet) over a medium–high heat. Add the cumin seeds and toast until warm to the touch and fragrant but not yet smoking. Pour into a mixing bowl. Place the coriander (cilantro), garlic and finger chilli in a pestle and mortar or small spice grinder and grind to a paste. Add to the cumin seeds. Now add the yoghurt, mango chutney and mint sauce and whisk until smooth. If it looks a bit thick, add a drop or two of milk to thin the raita to preference. Add sugar and salt to taste and place, covered, in the fridge until ready to serve. This will keep nicely, covered in the fridge, for at least 3 days.

PUNJABI TOMATO CHUTNEY

MAKES 250ML (1 CUP)

If you like Mexican food, you'll probably think this looks a lot like a Mexican tomato salsa. Then again, if you are a Punjabi food fan, you'll know this as a popular Punjabi sauce. They are the pretty much the same thing, so call it what you want. All I know is that it tastes great on nearly any Indian grilled chicken dish.

PREP TIME: 10 MINS

400g (14oz) tinned (canned) chopped tomatoes
1 small onion, roughly chopped
3 garlic cloves, smashed and roughly chopped
4 green chillies, chopped (more or less to taste)
1 small bunch of coriander (cilantro), chopped
Juice of about 2 limes
Salt, to taste

Place everything up to and including the coriander (cilantro) in a blender and blend until almost smooth. You still want to see some bits of onion, chillies and garlic in it. Taste this and add lime juice and salt to taste. Place in the fridge until required. This will keep in the fridge for at least 3 days.

GREEN CHILLI AND CORIANDER CHUTNEY

MAKES 385ML (1½ CUPS)

This is a versatile sauce that goes well with so many things, from grilled chicken to burgers to biryanis. I always have some of this in my fridge.

PREP TIME: 5 MINS

30g (1oz) coriander (cilantro), roughly chopped
10 mint leaves
Juice of 1 lemon or lime (to taste)
1 tsp salt, or to taste
½ tsp ground cumin
6 green finger chillies, roughly chopped
2 garlic cloves, roughly chopped
200g (about 1 cup) Greek yoghurt

Place all the ingredients in a blender, except for the yoghurt. Pulse a couple of times and then add about 2 tablespoons of the yoghurt. Now blend until you have a smooth paste. In a bowl, whisk the remaining yoghurt until smooth and then add the paste. Whisk it all together until you have a smooth sauce. Be sure to taste it and add more lemo or lime juice or salt to taste.

SUPPLIERS

I have personally used each of the following suppliers and had good service. Unless otherwise stated, I do not have any affiliation with them.

INGREDIENTS

SPICE KITCHEN ONLINE LTD

Spice Kitchen supplies excellent quality spices and has also begun producing Curry Guy-branded spice blends from my books, such as mixed powder, garam masala, tandoori masala and chaat masala. You can also order spice tins filled with whole spices or their own spice blends from around the world. If you are interested in making your own spice blends, co-owner Sanjay Aggarwal has an excellent new book out called *Spice Kitchen*.
www.spicekitchenuk.com

CEYLON SUPERMART

In addition to many ingredients used in Indian cuisine, Ceylon Supermart supplies a good range of Sri Lankan ingredients, such as dark-roasted curry powder and matta (raw red) rice.
www.ceylonsupermart.com

SPICES OF INDIA

In addition to groceries and spices, you will also find a fantastic range of kitchen and tableware.
www.spicesofindia.co.uk

THE ASIAN COOKSHOP

I normally purchase Asian ingredients locally but have used this company and like their service. You'll find pretty much everything you need for the Asian recipes in this book on this site.
www.theasiancookshop.co.uk

CHARCOAL

BIG K

I highly recommend the top-quality lumpwood charcoal, charcoal briquettes and kiln-dried logs supplied by Big K. **www.bigkproducts.co.uk**

BARBECUES & TANDOOR OVENS

WEBER

The Weber kettle barbecue is a great and reasonably priced barbecue for both indirect and direct heat cooking (see page 127). Not only is it perfect for cooking at home, but it is also easy to pack up and take with you when camping.
www.weber.com

THÜROS BARBECUES

If you love kebabs, you've got to check out the Thüros Kebab Grills. I love mine.
www.thueros.com

KAMADO JOE BARBECUES

Looking for a ceramic barbecue? I've tried many but the Kamado Joe is the one I love most!
https://kamadojoe.co.uk/

KADAI FIREBOWLS

A firebowl and barbecue in one! Perfect for grilling and cooking curries with a range of accessories. **www.kadai.co.uk**

TRAEGER BARBECUES

Traeger barbecues use wood pellets to cook the food. You can set the preferred temperature and then let the Traeger do all the work. This is the perfect barbecue for easy indirect cooking (see page 127). **www.traeger.com**

MEAT THERMOMETERS

THERMAPEN

When roasting and grilling, it's important to get the internal temperature of your meat right. For reliable thermometers visit:
www.thermapen.co.uk

MEATER THERMOMETER

Meater is a wireless smart meat thermometer that monitors cooking temperature, connecting to a mobile app for precise, remote monitoring. It's a fantastic product! **www.meater.com**

INDEX

A

almonds: chicken shahi korma 66
  Malai chicken seekh kebabs 136
ayam rica rica 57

B

baguettes: bánh mì 115
Bangalore green chilli chicken
  curry 65
bánh mì 115
barbecues 124–49
  how much fuel to use 127
  lighting 126
  oven cooking 127
  preparing for direct heat
    grilling 127
  preparing for indirect cooking 127
  setting up barbecues 126–7
bhuna karahi, chicken 43
biryani, Thai chicken 92
black pepper chicken karahi 48
breads: bánh mì 115
  chicken shami bun kebabs 118
  instant parathas 164
  keema pav 122
  naans 165
  rumali rotis 166
  tandoori chicken burger 117
  white chicken shahi kofta
    korma 68
broccoli: Korean miso chicken 106
bulgogi, chicken 128
burger, tandoori chicken 117
butter chicken: butter chicken
  karahi 35
  grilled butter chicken 130
buttermilk: Korean fried chicken
  kimbap 13

C

cabbage: soto ayam 58
carrots: carrot and radish pickle 115
  Korean fried chicken kimbap 13
cashews: dragon chicken 18
  makhani gravy 155
  white chicken shahi kofta
    korma 68

white gravy 158
chaap, Kolkata chicken 108
chana dal: chicken Haleem 94
changezi, chicken 71
chapli kebabs, chicken 100
cheese: bánh mì 115
  chicken shami bun kebabs 118
  da lat chicken pizza 15
chicken: ayam rica rica 57
  baked tandoori chicken wings 26
  Bangalore green chilli chicken
    curry 65
  bánh mì 115
  black pepper chicken karahi 48
  butter chicken karahi 35
  chicken bhuna karahi 43
  chicken bulgogi 128
  chicken changezi 71
  chicken chapli kebabs 100
  chicken chole karahi 44
  chicken floss 162
  chicken Frankie 121
  chicken Haleem 94
  chicken jalfrezi karahi 41
  chicken jali kebabs 105
  chicken karahi with chillies and
    garlic 33
  chicken keema karahi 38
  chicken lilit 148
  chicken majestic 16
  chicken namkeen karahi 51
  chicken pallipalayam 60
  chicken rendang 97
  chicken rogan josh 84
  chicken roghani 84
  chicken saag karahi 47
  chicken samosa cups 22
  chicken shahi korma 66
  chicken shami bun kebabs 118
  chicken shami kebabs 111
  chicken stock 160
  chicken yakitori 145
  crispy Indonesian fried
    chicken 102
  da lat chicken pizza 15
  dragon chicken 18
  General Tso's chicken 91

gilafi chicken seekh kebabs 138
Goan-style chicken vindaloo 79
grilled butter chicken 130
honey roast tandoori chicken 141
Indonesian chicken sate 133
Indonesian grilled chicken 146
jeera (cumin) chicken curry 55
kagzhi kebabs 135
kari ayam jawa 73
keema pav 122
Kolkata chicken chaap 108
Korean chicken stew 87
Korean fried chicken kimbap 13
Korean miso chicken 106
Korean spicy ramen 74
Malai chicken seekh kebabs 136
pandan chicken 24
Punjabi chicken samosas 21
Punjabi ginger chicken curry 81
soto ayam 58
South Indian chicken drumstick
  curry 63
Sri Lankan chicken curry 89
Szechuan chicken 76
tandoori chicken burger 117
Thai chicken biryani 92
Vietnamese-style rotisserie
  chicken 143
Vietnamese whole boiled
  chicken 82
white chicken karahi (korma) 36
white chicken shahi kofta
  korma 68
chicken fat, rendering 51
chicken majestic 16
chicken pâté: bánh mì 115
chickpeas: chicken chole karahi 44
chillies: ayam rica rica 57
  baked tandoori chicken wings 26
  Bangalore green chilli chicken
    curry 65
  chicken bhuna karahi 43
  chicken changezi 71
  chicken chapli kebabs 100
  chicken floss 162
  chicken jalfrezi karahi 41

chicken karahi with chillies and garlic 33
chicken keema karahi 38
chicken majestic 16
chicken namkeen karahi 51
chicken pallipalayam 60
chicken rendang 97
chicken samosa cups 22
chicken shahi korma 66
chicken shami kebabs 111
dipping sauce 13
General Tso's chicken 91
Goan-style chicken vindaloo 79
green chilli and coriander chutney 169
green sauce 118
hariyali (green) gravy 156
Indonesian chicken sate 133
Indonesian grilled chicken 146
jeera (cumin) chicken curry 55
keema pav 122
Kolkata chicken chaap 108
Korean spicy ramen 74
nu'ó'c châ'm 163
Punjabi chicken samosas 21
Punjabi tomato chutney 169
soto ayam 58
South Indian chicken drumstick curry 63
Szechuan chicken 76
tarka 94
Thai cucumber salad 163
white chicken karahi (korma) 36
white chicken shahi kofta korma 68
white gravy 158
chole karahi, chicken 44
chutney: green chilli and coriander chutney 169
Punjabi tomato chutney 169
coconut: chicken lilit 148
chicken pallipalayam 60
coconut (kerisik): chicken rendang 97
coconut milk: Bangalore green chilli chicken curry 65
chicken rendang 97
kari ayam jawa 73
South Indian chicken drumstick curry 63
Sri Lankan chicken curry 89

coriander (cilantro): all-purpose tandoori marinade 168
baked tandoori chicken wings 26
Bangalore green chilli chicken curry 65
chicken bhuna karahi 43
green chilli and coriander chutney 169
green sauce 118
hariyali (green) gravy 156
Punjabi tomato chutney 169
soto ayam 58
South Indian chicken drumstick curry 63
Thai chicken biryani 92
coriander seeds: garam masala 161
cracked wheat: chicken Haleem 94
cream: butter chicken karahi 35
white chicken karahi (korma) 36
crispy Indonesian fried chicken 102
cucumber: bánh mì 115
Korean fried chicken kimbap 13
Thai cucumber salad 163
cumin: garam masala 161
jeera (cumin) chicken curry 55
curry: ayam rica rica 57
Bangalore green chilli chicken curry 65
chicken changezi 71
chicken haleem 94
chicken pallipalayam 60
chicken rogan josh 84
chicken shahi korma 66
Goan-style chicken vindaloo 79
jeera (cumin) chicken curry 55
kari ayam jawa 73
keema pav 122
Punjabi ginger chicken curry 81
South Indian chicken drumstick curry 63
Sri Lankan chicken curry 89
Thai chicken biryani 92
white chicken shahi kofta korma 68

D

da lat chicken pizza 15
daikon: carrot and radish (daikon) pickle 115
dipping sauces 13

nu'ó'c châ'm 163
dragon chicken 18

E

eggs: chicken Frankie 121
chicken shami bun kebabs 118
Korean spicy ramen 74
soto ayam 58

F

fenugreek leaves: chicken saag karahi 47
filo pastry: chicken samosa cups 22
flavour, achieving optimum flavour in karahi cooking 31
floss, chicken 162
Frankie, chicken 121

G

garam masala 161
garlic: ayam rica rica 57
chicken chapli kebabs 100
chicken karahi with chillies and garlic 33
chicken lilit 148
chicken pallipalayam 60
chicken shami kebabs 111
crispy Indonesian fried chicken 102
garlic and ginger paste 161
Goan-style chicken vindaloo 79
Indonesian chicken sate 133
Indonesian grilled chicken 146
kari ayam jawa 73
Korean chicken stew 87
Malai chicken seekh kebabs 136
mint raita 168
soto ayam 58
South Indian chicken drumstick curry 63
Thai chicken biryani 92
Vietnamese-style rotisserie chicken 143
Vietnamese whole boiled chicken 82
General Tso's chicken 91
ghee 9
gilafi chicken seekh kebabs 138
ginger: garlic and ginger paste 161
Punjabi ginger chicken curry 81

South Indian chicken drumstick curry 63
tarka 94
white chicken karahi (korma) 36
Goan-style chicken vindaloo 79
gochugaru (Korean hot pepper flakes): Korean chicken stew 87
gochujang (Korean hot pepper paste): chicken bulgogi 128
Korean chicken stew 87
Korean miso chicken 106
Korean spicy ramen 74
gravies, Indian hotel (restaurant) 152–9
hariyali (green) gravy 156
how to use 152–3
makhani gravy 155
onion gravy 159
portion sizes 152
tailoring to tastes 153
tomato and onion gravy 154
upscaling and downscaling 153
white gravy 158
green chilli and coriander chutney 169
green sauce 118

H
Haleem, chicken 94
hariyali (green) gravy 156
honey roast tandoori chicken 141

I
Indonesian chicken sate 133
Indonesian fried chicken, crispy 102
Indonesian grilled chicken 146
Indonesian rice cakes 167

J
jalfrezi karahi, chicken 41
jeera (cumin) chicken curry 55

K
kagzhi kebabs 135
karahi cooking 28–51
achieving optimum flavour 31
black pepper chicken karahi 48
butter chicken karahi 35
chicken bhuna karahi 43
chicken chole karahi 44
chicken jalfrezi karahi 41

chicken karahi with chillies and garlic 33
chicken keema karahi 38
chicken namkeen karahi 51
chicken saag karahi 47
cooking the tomatoes 31
how much oil to use 30
karahi pans and substitutes 31
what karahi curries are 30
white chicken karahi (korma) 36
kari ayam jawa 73
kebabs: chicken chapli kebabs 100
chicken jali kebabs 105
chicken shami bun kebabs 118
chicken shami kebabs 111
gilafi chicken seekh kebabs 138
Indonesian chicken sate 133
kagzhi kebabs 135
Malai chicken seekh kebabs 136
see also skewers
keema: chicken keema karahi 38
chicken samosa cups 22
keema pav 122
kimbap, Korean fried chicken 13
koftas: white chicken shahi kofta korma 68
Kolkata chicken chaap 108
Korean chicken stew 87
Korean fried chicken kimbap 13
Korean miso chicken 106
Korean spicy ramen 74
korma: chicken shahi korma 66
white chicken karahi (korma) 36
white chicken shahi kofta korma 68

L
lemongrass: chicken floss 162
chicken lilit 148
chicken rendang 97
soto ayam 58
Vietnamese-style rotisserie chicken 143
Vietnamese whole boiled chicken 82
lentils: chicken shami kebabs 111
lettuce: bánh mì 115

M
makhani gravy 155
Malai chicken seekh kebabs 136

melon seeds: white gravy 158
mint: Bangalore green chilli chicken curry 65
green sauce 118
hariyali (green) gravy 156
mint raita 168
miso: Korean miso chicken 106
Korean spicy ramen 74
moong dal: chicken Haleem 94
mushrooms: Korean spicy ramen 74
mustard leaves: chicken saag karahi 47

N
naans 165
namkeen karahi, chicken 51
noodles: Korean spicy ramen 74
soto ayam 58
nu'ó'c châ'm 163

O
oil 9
how much to use in karahi cooking 30
serving oil-heavy dishes 9
onions: onion gravy 159
South Indian chicken drumstick curry 63
tomato and onion gravy 154
white gravy 158

P
pallipalayam, chicken 60
pandan chicken 24
paneer: kagzhi kebabs 135
panko breadcrumbs: chicken jali kebabs 105
Korean fried chicken kimbap 13
parathas, instant 164
pâté: bánh mì 115
peanuts: Indonesian chicken sate 133
peppercorns: black pepper chicken karahi 48
peppers: dragon chicken 18
gilafi chicken seekh kebabs 138
Kolkata chicken chaap 108
Szechuan chicken 76
pickle, carrot and radish 115
pizzas, da lat chicken 15
potatoes: Korean chicken stew 87

Punjabi chicken samosas 21
Punjabi ginger chicken curry 81
Punjabi tomato chutney 169

R
raita: mint raita 168
    spring onion raita 117
ramen, Korean spicy 74
red (masoor) dal: chicken
    Haleem 94
rendang, chicken 97
rice: Indonesian rice cakes 167
    Korean fried chicken kimbap 13
    steamed white basmati rice 164
    Thai chicken biryani 92
rice paper: da lat chicken pizza 15
rogan josh, chicken 84
roghani, chicken 84
rotis, rumali 166
rotisserie chicken, Vietnamese-
    style 143
rumali rotis 166

S
saag karahi, chicken 47
salad, Thai cucumber 163
samosas: chicken samosa cups 22
    Punjabi chicken samosas 21
sate, Indonesian chicken 133
seaweed: Korean fried chicken
    kimbap 13
seekh kebabs: gilafi chicken seekh
    kebabs 138
    Malai chicken seekh kebabs 136
shahi korma: chicken shahi
    korma 66
    white chicken shahi kofta
    korma 68
shallots: ayam rica rica 57
    chicken lilit 148
    chicken pallipalayam 60
    chicken rendang 97
    crispy Indonesian fried
    chicken 102
    Indonesian grilled chicken 146
    kari ayam jawa 73
    soto ayam 58
shami kebabs: chicken shami bun
    kebabs 118
    chicken shami kebabs 111
skewers: chicken lilit 148

chicken yakitori 145
soto ayam 58
South Indian chicken drumstick
    curry 63
soy sauce: dipping sauce 13
spices: garam masala 161
spinach: chicken saag karahi 47
    hariyali (green) gravy 156
split chana lentils: chicken shami
    kebabs 111
spring onions (scallions): chicken
    yakitori 145
    spring onion raita 117
Sri Lankan chicken curry 89
sriracha: chicken shami bun
    kebabs 118
stews, Korean chicken 87
stock, chicken 160
sushi rice: Korean fried chicken
    kimbap 13
sweet green peppers: Sri Lankan
    chicken curry 89
Szechuan chicken 76

T
tandoori chicken: all-purpose
    tandoori marinade 168
    baked tandoori chicken wings 26
    honey roast tandoori chicken 141
    tandoori chicken burger 117
tarka 94
Thai chicken biryani 92
Thai cucumber salad 163
tomatoes: Bangalore green chilli
    chicken curry 65
    bánh mì 115
    black pepper chicken karahi 48
    butter chicken karahi 35
    chicken bhuna karahi 43
    chicken changezi 71
    chicken chapli kebabs 100
    chicken chole karahi 44
    chicken jalfrezi karahi 41
    chicken karahi with chillies and
    garlic 33
    chicken keema karahi 38
    chicken namkeen karahi 51
    chicken saag karahi 47
    chicken samosa cups 22
    chicken shami bun kebabs 118
    cooking in karahi recipes 31

Goan-style chicken vindaloo 79
    makhani gravy 155
    Punjabi ginger chicken curry 81
    Punjabi tomato chutney 169
    soto ayam 58
    South Indian chicken drumstick
    curry 63
    tomato and onion gravy 154
tortillas: chicken Frankie 121

V
vermicelli: soto ayam 58
Vietnamese dipping sauce: nu'ó'c
    châ'm 163
Vietnamese-style rotisserie
    chicken 143
Vietnamese whole boiled chicken 82
vindaloo, Goan-style chicken 79

W
white chicken karahi (korma) 36
white chicken shahi kofta korma 68
white gravy 158
white urad dal: chicken Haleem 94
wraps: chicken Frankie 121

Y
yakitori, chicken 145
yoghurt: all-purpose tandoori
    marinade 168
    baked tandoori chicken wings 26
    black pepper chicken karahi 48
    butter chicken karahi 35
    chicken changezi 71
    chicken karahi with chillies and
    garlic 33
    chicken majestic 16
    chicken shahi korma 66
    green chilli and coriander
    chutney 169
    grilled butter chicken 130
    honey roast tandoori chicken 141
    keema pav 122
    mint raita 168
    Punjabi ginger chicken curry 81
    spring onion raita 117
    white chicken karahi (korma) 36
    white gravy 158

ACKNOWLEDGEMENTS

It was a pleasure to work with everyone at Quadrille to produce this book. It's a big team effort. Thank you to Sarah Lavelle for commissioning the project and to my editor, Vicky Orchard, for all her help with my words and for bringing this book together. Thank you also Katy Everett for coordinating it all.

Thanks to Kris Kirkham, who has worked with me on every cookbook I've written, and food stylist Rosie Reynolds, for bringing my recipes to life in a way that only they can. Thank you also to Kris's assistant, Phoebe Pearson, and Rosie's assistant cooks: Emma Cantlay, Stevie Taylor and Antonia Bellini. We could not have done it without them!

A big thank you goes out to the moderators of my Facebook group: Jon Monday, Steven Lumsden, Tim Martin, Karen Bolan, Claire Rees, Anne-Marie Goodfellow, James Vaisey and Derek Turnbull. Your help and support is so much appreciated.

Thank you to props stylist Faye Wears, who sourced the props and dishes. They were perfect!

Thank you to my agent, Clare Hulton, for all her support and for once again making things happen.

I could not have written this book without my wife Caroline's support. She helped cook every recipe to ensure that the recipes worked and tasted as they should. Together we not only write recipes for my books but test them first on the blog.

I would also like to thank my son Joe Toombs and his fiancé, Shannon Ellerton, for their help with the recipes. They cooked and tested most, if not all, of these recipes and filmed many of them being made for my blog and social media. Their feedback and help perfecting these recipes for the home cook has been invaluable. They read and prepared each recipe as written, sometimes catching problems I didn't want going in a printed book. Thank you!

One last big thank you, and that goes out to you for picking up this book. I appreciate it so much and hope you enjoy the book and recipes as much as I enjoyed putting this collection together.

Managing Director: Sarah Lavelle
Project Editor: Vicky Orchard
Designer: Katy Everett
Cover Design: Smith & Gilmour
Photographer: Kris Kirkham
Photography Assistant: Phoebe Pearson
Food Stylist: Rosie Reynolds
Food Stylist Assistants: Emma Cantlay,
Stevie Taylor and Antonia Bellini
Props Stylist: Faye Wears
Head of Production: Stephen Lang
Production Controller: Sabeena Atchia

First published in 2024 by Quadrille
Publishing Limited

Quadrille
52–54 Southwark Street,
London SE1 1UN
quadrille.com

Text © 2024 Dan Toombs
Photography © 2024 Kris Kirkham
Design and layout © 2024 Quadrille

Cataloguing-in-Publication Data. A catalogue record for this book is available from the British Library.

ISBN 9781837831036

Printed in China

In five short years Dan took The Curry Guy from an idea to a reliable brand. The recipes are all developed and tested in Dan's home kitchen. And they work. His bestselling first cookbook – *The Curry Guy* – and the 750,000 curry fans who visit his blog www.greatcurryrecipes.net every month can testify to that fact.

If you have any recipe questions you can contact Dan (@thecurryguy) on X, Facebook or Instagram.